Goals!

GOALS!

*How to Get Everything
You Want—Faster Than You
Ever Thought Possible*

Brian Tracy

BK

BERRETT-KOEHLER PUBLISHERS, INC.
San Francisco

Berrett-Koehler Publishers, Inc.
235 Montgomery Street, Suite 650
San Francisco, CA 94104-2916
Tel: (415) 288-0260   Fax: (415) 362-2512   www.bkconnection.com

Ordering Information

Quantity sales. Special discounts are available on quantity purchases by corporations, associations, and others. For details, contact the "Special Sales Department" at the Berrett-Koehler address above.

Individual sales. Berrett-Koehler publications are available through most bookstores. They can also be ordered direct from Berrett-Koehler: Tel: (800) 929-2929; Fax: (802) 864-7626; www.bkconnection.com

Orders for college textbook/course adoption use. Please contact Berrett-Koehler: Tel: (800) 929-2929; Fax: (802) 864-7626.

Orders by U.S. trade bookstores and wholesalers. Please contact Publishers Group West, 1700 Fourth Street, Berkeley, CA 94710. Tel: (510) 528-1444; Fax (510) 528-3444.

Berrett-Koehler and the BK logo are registered trademarks of Berrett-Koehler Publishers, Inc.

Printed in the United States of America

Berrett-Koehler books are printed on long-lasting acid-free paper. When it is available, we choose paper that has been manufactured by environmentally responsible processes. These may include using trees grown in sustainable forests, incorporating recycled paper, minimizing chlorine in bleaching, or recycling the energy produced at the paper mill.

Library of Congress Cataloging-in-Publication Data
Tracy, Brian.
  Goals! : how to get everything you want—faster than you ever thought possible / by Brian Tracy.
    p. cm.
  Includes bibliographical referencs and index.
  ISBN-10: 1-57675-235-6; ISBN-13: 978-1-57675-235-7 (hardcover)
  ISBN-10: 1-57675-307-7; ISBN-13: 978-1-57675-307-1 (paperback)
  1. Goal (Psychology) 2. Success—Psychological aspects.
  I. Title.
BF505.G6 T73 2002
158.1—dc21   2002038318

Copyediting by PeopleSpeak.
Book design and composition by Beverly Butterfield, Girl of the West Productions.

FIRST EDITION
10 09 08 07 06   10 9 8 7 6 5 4

Contents

To Rick Metcalfe, a good friend,
a loving husband and father,
a great American, an extraordinary entrepreneur,
one of the best salesmen who ever lived, and
an inspiration to everyone who knew him.

I only wish you could be here to
read this book. You left us all too soon.

Preface

This book is for ambitious people who want to get ahead faster. If this is the way you think and feel, you are the person for whom this book is written. The ideas contained in the pages ahead will save you years of hard work in achieving the goals that are most important to you.

I have spoken more than two thousand times before audiences of as many as twenty-three thousand people in twenty-four countries. My seminars and talks have varied in length from five minutes to five days. In every case, I have focused on sharing the best ideas I could find on the particular subject with that audience at that moment. After countless talks on various themes, if I was given only five minutes to speak to you and I could convey only one thought that would help you to be more successful, I would tell you "Write down your goals, make plans to achieve them, and work on your plans every single day."

This advice, if you followed it, would be of more help to you than anything else you could ever learn. Many university graduates have told me that this simple concept has been more valuable to them than four years of study. This idea has changed my life and the lives of millions of other people. It will change yours as well.

The Turning Point

A group of successful men got together in Chicago some time ago to talk about the experiences of their lives. All of them were millionaires and multimillionaires. Like most successful people, they were both humble and grateful for what they had achieved and for the blessings that life had bestowed upon them. As they discussed the reasons why they had managed to achieve so much in life, the wisest man among them spoke up and said that, in his estimate, "success is goals, and all else is commentary."

Your time and your life are precious. The biggest waste of time and life is for you to spend years accomplishing something that you could have achieved in only a few months. By following the practical, proven process of goal setting and goal achieving laid out in this book, you will be able to accomplish vastly more in a shorter period of time than you have ever imagined before. The speed at which you move onward and upward will amaze both you and all the people around you.

By following these simple and easy-to-apply methods and techniques, you can move quickly from rags to riches in the months and years ahead. You can transform your experience from one of poverty and frustration to one of affluence and satisfaction. You can go far beyond your friends and family and achieve more in life than most other people you know.

In my talks, seminars, and consulting, I have worked with more than two million people all around the world. I have found, over and over, that a person of average intelligence with clear goals will run circles around a genius who is not sure what he or she really wants.

My personal mission statement has not changed in years. It is "To help people achieve their goals faster than they ever would in the absence of my help."

This book contains the distilled essence of all that I have learned in the areas of success, achievement, and goal attainment. By following the steps explained in the pages ahead, you will move to the front of the line in life. For my children, this book is meant to be a road map and a guide to help you get from wherever you are to wherever you want to go. For my friends and readers of this book, my reason for writing it is to give you a proven system that you can use to move onto the fast-track in your own life.

Welcome! A great new adventure is about to begin.

Introduction

This is a wonderful time to be alive. There have never been more opportunities for creative and determined people to achieve more of their goals than there are today. Regardless of short-term ups and downs in the economy and in your life, we are entering into an age of peace and prosperity superior to any previous era in human history.

In the year 1900, there were five thousand millionaires in America. By the year 2000, the number of millionaires had increased to more than five million, most of them self-made, in one generation. Experts predict that another ten to twenty million millionaires will be created in the next two decades. Your goal should be to become one of them. This book will show you how.

A Slow Start

When I was eighteen, I left high school without graduating. My first job was as a dishwasher in the back of a small hotel. From there, I moved on to washing cars and then washing floors with a janitorial service. For the next few years, I drifted and worked at various laboring jobs, earning my living by the sweat of my brow. I worked in sawmills and factories. I worked on farms and ranches. I worked in the tall timber with a chain saw and dug wells when the logging season ended.

I worked as a construction laborer on tall buildings and as a seaman on a Norwegian freighter in the North Atlantic. Often I slept in my car or in cheap rooming houses. When I was twenty-three, I worked as an itinerant farm laborer during the harvest, sleeping on hay in the barn and eating with the farmer's family. I was uneducated and unskilled, and at the end of the harvest I was unemployed once more.

When I could no longer find a laboring job, I got a job in straight commission sales, cold-calling office-to-office and door-to-door. I would often work all day long to make a single sale so that I could pay for my rooming house and have a place to sleep that night. This was not a great start at life.

The Day My Life Changed

Then one day, I took out a piece of paper and wrote down an outrageous goal for myself. It was to earn $1,000 per month in door-to-door and office-to-office selling. I folded up the piece of paper, put it away, and never found it again.

But thirty days later, my entire life had changed. During that time, I discovered a technique for closing sales that tripled my income from the very first day. Meanwhile, the owner of my company sold out to an entrepreneur who had just moved into town. Exactly thirty days after I had written down my goal, the new owner took me aside and offered me $1,000 per month to head up the sales force and teach the other salespeople what I was doing that enabled me to sell so much more than anyone else. I accepted his offer and from that day forward, my life was never the same.

Within eighteen months, I had moved from that job to another and then to another. I went from personal selling to becoming a sales manager with people selling for me. I recruited and built a ninety-five-person sales force. I went literally from worrying about my next meal to walking around with a pocket full of $20 bills.

I began teaching my salespeople how to write out their goals and how to sell more effectively. In almost no time at all, they increased their incomes as much as tenfold. Today, many of them are millionaires and multimillionaires.

It's important to note that since those days in my mid-twenties, my life has not been a smooth series of upward steps. It has included many ups and downs, marked by occasional successes and temporary failures. I have traveled, lived, and worked in more than eighty countries, learning French, German, and Spanish along the way and working in twenty-two different fields.

As the result of inexperience and sometimes sheer stupidity, I have spent or lost everything I made and had to start over again—several times. Whenever this happened, I would begin by sitting down with a piece of paper and laying out a new set of goals for myself, using the methods that I'll explain in the pages ahead.

After several years of hit-and-miss goal setting and goal achieving, I finally decided to collect everything I had learned into a single system. By assembling these ideas and strategies in one place, I developed a goal-setting methodology and process, with a beginning, middle, and end, and began to follow it every day.

Within one year, my life had changed once more. In January of that year, I was living in a rented apartment with rented furniture. I was $35,000 in debt and driving a used car that wasn't paid for. By December, I was living in my own $100,000 condominium. I owned a new Mercedes, had paid off all my debts, and had $50,000 in the bank.

Then I really got serious about success. I realized that goal setting was incredibly powerful. I invested hundreds and then thousands of hours reading and researching goal setting and goal achieving, synthesizing the best ideas I could find into a complete process that worked with incredible effectiveness.

Anyone Can Do It

In 1981, I began teaching my system in workshops and seminars that have now reached more than two million people in thirty-five countries. I began audiotaping and videotaping my courses so that others could use them. We have now trained hundreds of thousands of people in these principles, in multiple languages, all over the world.

What I found was that these ideas work everywhere, for everyone, in virtually every country, no matter what your education, experience, or background may be when you begin.

Best of all, these ideas have made it possible for me and many thousands of others to take complete control over our lives. The regular and systematic practice of goal setting has taken us from poverty to prosperity, from frustration to fulfillment, from underachievement to success and satisfaction. This system will do the same for you.

What I learned early on is that any plan is better than no plan at all. And it is not necessary to reinvent the wheel. All the answers have already been found. Hundreds of thousands and perhaps even millions of men and women have started with nothing and achieved great success following these principles. And what others have done, you can do as well if you just learn how.

In the pages ahead, you will learn twenty-one of the most important ideas and strategies ever discovered for achieving everything that you could ever want in life. You will find that there are no limits to what you can accomplish except for the limits you place on your own imagination. And since there are no limits to what you can imagine, there are no limits to what you can achieve. This is one of the greatest discoveries of all. Let us begin.

> A journey of a thousand leagues
> begins with a single step.
> —CONFUCIUS

1

Unlock Your Potential

The potential of the average person is like a huge ocean unsailed, a new continent unexplored, a world of possibilities waiting to be released and channeled toward some great good.

—BRIAN TRACY

Success is goals, and all else is commentary. All successful people are intensely goal oriented. They know what they want and they are focused single-mindedly on achieving it, every single day.

Your ability to set goals is the master skill of success. Goals unlock your positive mind and release ideas and energy for goal attainment. Without goals, you simply drift and flow on the currents of life. With goals, you fly like an arrow, straight and true to your target.

The truth is that you probably have more natural potential than you could use if you lived one hundred lifetimes. Whatever you have accomplished up until now is only a small fraction of what is truly possible for you. One of the rules for success is this: It doesn't matter where you're coming from; all that matters is where you're going. And where you are going is solely determined by yourself and your own thoughts.

Clear goals increase your confidence, develop your competence, and boost your levels of motivation. As sales trainer Tom Hopkins says, "Goals are the fuel in the furnace of achievement."

You Create Your Own World

Perhaps the greatest discovery in human history is the power of your mind to create almost every aspect of your life. Everything you see around you in the man-made world began as a thought or an idea in the mind of a single person before it was translated into reality. Everything in your life started as a thought, a wish, a hope, or a dream either in your mind or in the mind of someone else. Your thoughts are creative. Your thoughts form and shape your world and everything that happens to you.

The great summary statement of all religions, all philosophies, metaphysics, psychology, and success is this: **You become what you think about most of the time.** Your outer world ultimately becomes a reflection of your inner world and mirrors back to you what you think about. Whatever you think about continuously emerges in your reality.

Many thousands of successful people have been asked what they think about most of the time. The most common answer given by successful people is that they think about *what they want,* and *how to get it* most of the time.

Unsuccessful, unhappy people think and talk about what they don't want most of the time. They talk about their problems and worries and who is to blame most of the time. But successful people keep their thoughts and conversations on the topics of their most intensely desired goals. They think and talk about what they want most of the time.

Living without clear goals is like driving in a thick fog. No matter how powerful or well engineered your car, you drive slowly, hesitantly, making little progress on even the smoothest road. Deciding upon your goals clears the fog immediately and allows you to focus and channel your energies and abilities. Clear goals enable you to step on the accelerator of your own life and race ahead rapidly toward achieving more of what you really want.

Your Automatic Goal-Seeking Function

Imagine this exercise: You take a homing pigeon out of its roost, put it in a cage, cover the cage with a blanket, put the cage in a box, and then place the box into a closed truck cab. You can then drive a thousand miles in any direction. If you then open the truck cab, take out the box, take off the blanket, and let the homing pigeon out of the cage, the homing pigeon will fly up into the air, circle three times, and then fly unerringly back to its home roost a thousand miles away. No other creature on Earth has this incredible cybernetic, goal-seeking function except for man.

You have the same goal-achieving ability as the homing pigeon but with one marvelous addition. When you are absolutely clear about your goal, you do not even have to know where it is or how to achieve it. By simply deciding exactly what you want, you will begin to move unerringly toward your goal, and your goal will start to move unerringly toward you. At exactly the right time and in exactly the right place, you and the goal will meet.

Because of this incredible cybernetic mechanism located deep within your mind, you almost always achieve your goals, whatever they are. If your goal is to get home at night and watch television, you will almost certainly achieve it. If your goal is to create a wonderful life full of health, happiness, and prosperity, you will achieve that as well. Like a computer, your goal-seeking mechanism is nonjudgmental. It works automatically and continuously to bring you what you want, regardless of what you program into it.

Nature doesn't care about the size of your goals. If you set little goals, your automatic goal-achieving mechanism will enable you to achieve little goals. If you set large goals, this natural capability will enable you to achieve large goals. The size, scope, and detail of the goals you choose to think about most of the time are completely up to you.

Why People Don't Set Goals

Here is a good question: If goal seeking is automatic, why do so few people have clear, written, measurable, time-bounded goals that they work toward each day? This is one of the great mysteries of life. I believe there are four reasons why people don't set goals.

They Think Goals Aren't Important

First, most people don't realize the importance of goals. If you grow up in a home where no one has goals or you socialize with a group where goals are neither discussed nor valued, you can very easily reach adulthood without knowing that your ability to set and achieve goals will have more of an effect on your life than any other skill. Look around you. How many of your friends or family members are clear and committed to their goals?

They Don't Know How

The second reason that people don't have goals is because they don't know how to set them in the first place. Even worse, many people think that they already have goals when what they actually have is a series of wishes or dreams, like

"Be happy" or "Make a lot of money" or "Have a nice family life."

But these are not goals at all. They are merely fantasies that are common to everyone. A goal, however, is something distinctly different from a wish. It is clear, written, and specific. It can be quickly and easily described to another person. You can measure it, and you know when you have achieved it or not.

It is possible to earn an advanced degree at a leading university without ever receiving *one hour* of instruction on goal setting. It is almost as if the people who determine the educational content of our schools and universities are completely blind to the importance of goal setting in achieving success later in life. And of course, if you never hear about goals until you are an adult, as I experienced, you will have no idea how important they are to everything you do.

They Have a Fear of Failure

The third reason that people don't set goals is because of the fear of failure. Failure *hurts*. It is emotionally and often financially painful and distressing. Everyone has experienced failure from time to time. Each time, we resolve to be more careful and avoid failure in the future. Many people then make the mistake of unconsciously sabotaging themselves by not setting any goals at which they might fail. They end up going through life functioning at far lower levels than are truly possible for them.

They Have a Fear of Rejection

The fourth reason that people don't set goals is because of the fear of rejection. People are afraid that if they set a goal and are not successful, others will criticize or ridicule them. This is one of the reasons why you should keep your goals confidential when you begin to set goals. Don't tell anyone. Let others see what you have accomplished, but don't tell them in advance. What they don't know can't hurt you.

Join the Top 3 Percent

Mark McCormack in his book *What They Don't Teach You at Harvard Business School* tells of a Harvard study conducted between 1979 and 1989. In 1979, the graduates of the MBA program at Harvard were asked, "Have you set clear, written goals for your future and made plans to accomplish them?" It turned out that only 3 percent of the graduates had written goals and plans. Thirteen percent had goals, but they were not in writing. Fully 84 percent had no specific goals at all, aside from getting out of school and enjoying the summer.

Ten years later, in 1989, the researchers interviewed the members of that class again. They found that the 13 percent who had goals that were not in writing were earning, on average, twice as much as the 84 percent of students who had no goals at all. But most surprisingly, they found that the 3 percent of graduates who had clear, written goals when they left Harvard were earning, on average, *ten times* as much as the other 97 percent of graduates *all together.* The only difference between the groups was the clarity of the goals they had for themselves when they graduated.

No Road Signs

The importance of clarity is easy to understand. Imagine arriving on the outskirts of a large city and being told to drive to a particular home or office in that city. But here's the catch: There are no road signs and you have no map of the city. In fact, all you are given is a very general description of the home or office. The question is, How long do you think it would take you to find the home or office in the city without a road map and without road signs?

The answer is, Probably your whole life. If you ever did find the home or office, it would be very much a matter of luck. And sadly enough, this is the way most people live their lives.

Most people start life traveling aimlessly through an un-mapped and uncharted world. This is the equivalent of starting off in life with no goals and plans. They simply figure things out as they go along. Often, ten or twenty years of work will go past and they will still be broke, unhappy in their jobs, dissatisfied with their marriages and making little progress. And still, they will go home every night and watch television, wishing and hoping that things will get better. But they seldom do. Not by themselves.

Happiness Requires Goals

Earl Nightingale once wrote, "Happiness is the progressive realization of a worthy ideal, or goal."

You feel truly happy only when you are making progress, step-by-step, toward something that is important to you. Victor Frankl, the founder of logotherapy, wrote that the greatest need of human beings is for *a sense of meaning and purpose in life.*

Goals give you a sense of meaning and purpose. Goals give you a sense of direction. As you move toward your goals you feel happier and stronger. You feel more energized and effective. You feel more competent and confident in yourself and your abilities. Every step you take toward your goals increases your belief that you can set and achieve even bigger goals in the future.

More people today fear change and worry about the future than at any other time in our history. One of the great benefits of goal setting is that goals enable you to *control the direction of change* in your life. Goals enable you to assure that the changes in your life are largely self-determined and self-directed. Goals enable you to instill meaning and purpose into everything you do.

One of the most important teachings of Aristotle, the Greek philosopher, was that man is a teleological organism. The Greek word *teleos* means *goals*. Aristotle concluded that all human action is purposeful in some way. You are happy only when you are doing something that is moving you toward something that you want. The great questions then become, What are your goals? What purposes are you aiming at? Where do you want to end up at the end of the day?

Clarity Is Everything

Your inborn potential is extraordinary. You have within you, right now, the ability to achieve almost any goal that you can set for yourself. Your greatest responsibility to yourself is to invest whatever time is required to become absolutely clear about exactly what you want and how you can best achieve it. The greater clarity you have regarding your true goals, the more of your potential you will unleash for good in your life.

You have probably heard it said that the average person uses only 10 percent of his or her potential. The sad fact is that, according to Stanford University, the average person functions with only about 2 percent of his or her mental potential. The remainder just sits there in reserve, being saved for some later time. This would be exactly as if your parents had left you a trust fund with $100,000 in it but all you ever took out to spend was $2,000. The other $98,000 simply sat in the account, unused throughout your life.

Develop a Burning Desire

The starting point of all goal attainment is *desire*. You must develop an intense burning desire for your goals if you really want to achieve them. Only when your desire becomes intense enough will you have the energy and the internal drive to overcome all the obstacles that will arise in your path.

The good news is that almost anything that you want long enough and hard enough, you can ultimately achieve.

The great oil billionaire H. L. Hunt was once asked the secret of success. He replied that success required two things and two things only. First, he said, you must know *exactly* what you want. Most people never make this decision. Second, he said, you must determine the *price* that you will have to pay to achieve it and then get busy paying that price.

The Cafeteria Model of Success

Life is more like a buffet or cafeteria than a restaurant. In a restaurant, you eat the complete meal and then you pay the bill. But in a buffet or cafeteria, you have to serve yourself and pay in full before you enjoy the meal. Many people make the mistake of thinking that they will pay the price *after* they have experienced success. They sit in front of the stove of life and say, "First give me some heat, and then I'll put in some wood."

As motivational speaker Zig Ziglar once said, "The elevator to success is out of service. But the stairs are always open."

Another important observation from Aristotle was his conclusion that the ultimate purpose of all human action is the achievement of personal happiness. Whatever you do, he said, it is aimed at increasing your happiness in some way. You may or may not be successful in achieving happiness, but your happiness is always your ultimate aim.

The Key to Happiness

Setting goals, working toward them day by day, and ultimately achieving them is the key to happiness in life. Goal setting is so powerful that the very act of *thinking* about your goals makes you happy, even before you have taken the first step toward achieving them.

To unlock and unleash your full potential, you should make a habit of daily goal setting and achieving for the rest of your life. You should develop a laser-like focus so that you are always thinking and talking about what you want rather than what you don't want. You must resolve, from this moment on, to be a goal-seeking organism, like a guided missile or a homing pigeon, moving unerringly toward the goals that are important to you.

There is no greater guarantee of a long, happy, healthy, and prosperous life than for you to be continually working on being, having, and achieving more and more of the things you really want. Clear goals enable you to release your full potential for personal and professional success. Goals enable you to overcome any obstacle and to make your future achievement unlimited.

❖ UNLOCK YOUR POTENTIAL

1 Imagine that you have the inborn ability to achieve any goal you could ever set for yourself. What do you really want to be, have, and do?

2 What are the activities that give you your greatest sense of meaning and purpose in life?

3 Look at your personal and work life today and identify how your own thinking has created your world. What should you or could you change?

4 What do you think and talk about most of the time—what you want or what you don't want?

5 What is the price you will have to pay to achieve the goals that are most important to you?

6 What one action should you take immediately as the result of your answers to the above questions?

2

Take Charge of Your Life

A man, as a general rule, owes very little to what he is born with—a man is what he makes of himself.

—ALEXANDER GRAHAM BELL

When I was twenty-one, I was broke and living in a small one-room apartment in the middle of a very cold winter, working on a construction job during the day. In the evening, I usually couldn't afford to go out of my apartment, where at least it was warm, so I had a lot of time to think.

One night as I sat at my small kitchen table, I had a great flash of awareness. It changed my life. I suddenly realized that everything that would happen to me for the rest of my life was going to be up to me. No one else was ever going to help me. *No one was coming to the rescue.*

I was thousands of miles from home with no intentions of going back for a long time. I saw clearly at that moment that if anything in my life were going to change, it would have to begin with me. If I didn't change, nothing else would change. I was responsible.

The Great Discovery

I still remember that moment. It was like a first parachute jump—both scary and exhilarating. There I was, standing on the edge of life. And I decided to jump. From that moment onward, I accepted that I was in charge of my life. I knew that if I wanted my situation to be different, I would have to be different. Everything was up to me.

I later learned that when you accept complete responsibility for your life, you take the giant step from childhood to adulthood. Sadly enough, most people never do this. I have met countless men and women in their forties and fifties who are still grumbling and complaining about earlier unhappy experiences and still blaming their problems on other people and circumstances. Many people are still angry about something that one of their parents did or did not do to or for them twenty or thirty or even forty years ago. They are trapped in the past and they can't get free.

Your Worst Enemies

The greatest enemies of success and happiness are *negative emotions* of all kinds. Negative emotions hold you down, tire you out, and take away all your joy in life. Negative emotions, from the beginning of time, have done more harm to individuals and societies than all the plagues of history.

One of your most important goals, if you want to be truly happy and successful, is to free yourself from negative emotions. Fortunately, you can do this if you learn how.

The negative emotions of fear, self-pity, envy, jealousy, feelings of inferiority, and ultimately *anger* are mostly caused by four factors. Once you identify and remove these factors from your thinking, your negative emotions stop automatically. When your negative emotions stop, the positive emotions of love, peace, joy, and enthusiasm flow in to replace them, and your whole life changes for the better, sometimes in a matter of minutes or even seconds.

Stop Justifying

The first of the four root causes of negative emotions is *justi-fication.* You can be negative only as long as you can justify to yourself and others that you are *entitled* to be angry or upset for some reason. This is why angry people are continually explaining and elaborating on the reasons for their negative feelings. However, if you cannot *justify* your negativity, you cannot be angry.

For example, a person is laid off from a job due to a change in the economy and declining sales in the company. However, the individual is angry with his boss for this decision and justifies his anger by describing all the reasons why his being laid off is unfair. He can even get himself so incensed that he decides to sue or get even in some way. As long as he continues to justify his negative feelings toward his boss and the company, his negative emotions control him and occupy much of his life and thinking.

However, as soon as he says, "Well, I've been laid off. These things happen. It's not personal. People get laid off all the time. I guess I'd better get busy finding a new job," his negative emotions vanish. He becomes calm, clear, and focused on the goal and on the steps he can take to get back into the workforce. As soon as he stops justifying, he becomes a more positive and effective person.

Refuse to Rationalize and Make Excuses

The second cause of negative emotions is *rationalization.* When you rationalize, you attempt to give a "socially acceptable explanation for an otherwise socially unacceptable act."

You rationalize to explain away or put a favorable light on something that you have done that you feel bad or unhappy about. You excuse your actions by creating an explanation that *sounds good,* even though you know that you were an active agent in whatever occurred. You often create complex ways of putting yourself in the right by explaining that your behavior was really quite acceptable, all things considered. This rationalizing keeps your negative emotions alive.

Rationalization and justification always require that you make someone or something else the source or cause of your problem. You cast yourself in the role of the victim, and you make the other person or organization into the oppressor or the "bad guy."

Rise above the Opinions of Others

The third cause of negative emotions is an overconcern or a hypersensitivity about the way other people treat you. For some people, their entire self-image is determined by the way other people speak to them, talk to them or about them, or even look at them. They have little sense of personal value or self-worth apart from the opinions of others, and if those opinions are negative for any reason, real or imagined, the "victim" immediately experiences anger, embarrassment, shame, feelings of inferiority, and even depression, self-pity, and despair. This explains why psychologists say that almost everything we do is to earn the respect of others or at least to avoid *losing* their respect.

Realize That No One Else Is Responsible

The fourth cause of negative emotions, and the worst of all, is *blaming.* When I draw the "Negative Emotions Tree" in my seminars, I illustrate the trunk of the tree as the propensity to blame other people for our problems. Once you cut down the trunk of the tree, all the fruits of the tree—all the other negative emotions—die immediately, just as all the lights go out instantly when you jerk the plug out of the socket that lights up the bulbs on a Christmas tree.

Responsibility Is the Antidote

The antidote for negative emotions of all kinds is for you to accept complete responsibility for your situation. You cannot say the words "I am responsible!" and still feel angry. The very act of accepting responsibility short-circuits and cancels out any negative emotions you may be experiencing.

The discovery of this simple but powerful affirmation, "I am responsible," and its instant ability to eliminate negative emotions was a turning point in my life, as it has been for many hundreds of thousands of my students.

Just imagine! You can free yourself from negative emotions and begin taking control of your life by simply saying, "I am responsible!" whenever you start to feel angry or upset for any reason.

It is only when you free yourself from negative emotions, by taking complete responsibility, that you can begin to set and achieve goals in every area of your life. It is only when you are *free*, mentally and emotionally, that you can begin to channel your energies and enthusiasms in a forward direction. Without the acceptance of complete personal responsibility, no progress is possible. On the other hand, once you accept total responsibility for your life, there are no limits on what you can be, do, and have.

Stop Blaming Others

From now on, refuse to blame anyone for anything—past, present, or future. As Eleanor Roosevelt said, "No one can make you feel inferior without your consent." Buddy Hackett, the comedian, once said, "I never hold grudges; while you're holding grudges, they're out dancing!"

From this point forward, refuse to make excuses or to justify your behaviors. If you make a mistake, say, "I'm sorry," and get busy rectifying the situation. Every time you blame someone else or make excuses, you give your power away. You feel weakened and diminished. You feel negative and angry inside. Refuse to do it.

Control Your Emotions

To keep your mind positive, refuse to criticize, complain about, or condemn other people for anything. Every time you criticize someone else, complain about something you don't like, or condemn someone else for something that they have done or not done, you trigger feelings of negativity and anger within yourself. And you are the one who suffers. Your negativity doesn't affect the other person at all. Being angry with someone is allowing him or her to control your emotions, and often the entire quality of your life, at long distance. This is just plain silly.

Remember, as Gary Zukav says in his book *Seat of the Soul,* "Positive emotions empower; negative emotions disempower." Positive emotions of happiness, excitement, love, and enthusiasm make you feel more powerful and confident. Negative emotions of anger, hurt, or blame weaken you and make you hostile, irritable, and unpleasant to be around.

Once you decide to accept complete responsibility for yourself, your situation, and everything that happens to you, you can turn confidently toward your work and the affairs of your life. You become "the master of your fate and the captain of your soul."

Hello, Mr. President!

In a study done in New York some years ago, researchers found that people who ranked in the top 3 percent in every field had a special attitude that set them apart from average performers in their industries. It was this: they viewed themselves as *self-employed* throughout their careers, no matter who signed their paychecks. They saw themselves as responsible for their companies, exactly as if they owned the companies personally. You should do the same.

From this moment forward, see yourself as the president of your own personal services corporation. View yourself as self-employed. See yourself as being in complete charge of every part of your life and career. Remind yourself that you are where you are and what you are because of what you have done or failed to do. You are very much the architect of your own destiny.

You Choose, You Decide

You have determined your entire life up to now by the choices and decisions you have made or *failed* to make. If there is anything in your life that you don't like, you are responsible. If there is anything that you are unhappy about, it is up to you to take the necessary steps to change and improve it so that it is more to your liking.

As the president of your own personal services corporation, you are completely responsible for everything you do and for the results of what you do. You are responsible for the consequences of your actions and your behaviors. You are where you are and what you are today because you have decided to be there.

In a large sense, you are earning today exactly what you have decided to earn, no more and no less. If you are not happy with your current income, decide to earn more. Set it as a goal, make a plan, and get busy doing what you need to do to earn what you want to earn.

As the president of your own career and your own life, as the architect of your own destiny, you are free to make your own decisions. You are the boss. You are in charge.

Develop Your Own Strategy

Just as the president of a corporation is responsible for the strategy and activities of that corporation, you are responsible for the personal strategic planning of your own life and career. You are responsible for overall management strategy—setting goals, making plans, establishing measures, and performing to get results.

You are responsible for achieving certain outputs—the quality and quantity of the work that you produce and the results you are expected to get.

As president, you are responsible for marketing strategy—self-promotion and advancement, creating your image, and packaging yourself to be able to sell yourself for the very highest price in a competitive market.

You are responsible for financial strategy—for deciding exactly how much of your services you want to sell, how much you want to earn, how rapidly you want to grow your income year by year, how much you want to save and invest, and how much you want to be worth when you retire. These numbers are entirely up to you.

You are responsible for your people strategy and your relationships, both at home and at work. One piece of advice

I give my students is to "choose your boss with care." Your choice of a boss is going to have a major impact on how much you earn, how fast you get ahead, and how happy you will be at your job.

Make New Choices, New Decisions

By the same token, your choice of a mate and friends will have as much or more to do with your success and happiness than any other decisions you make. If you are not happy with any of your current choices, it is up to you to begin taking steps to improve or change them.

Finally, as president, you are in complete charge of personal research and development, personal training and learning. It is up to you to determine the talents, skills, abilities, and core competencies you will need to earn the kind of money you want to earn in the months and years ahead. It is then your responsibility to make the investment and take the time to learn and develop these skills. No one is going to do it for you. The unavoidable truth is that no one really cares as much as you do.

Become a "Growth Stock"

To take this analogy a little further, see yourself as a company with a stock that trades on the market. Could people invest in your stock and be confident that it will continue to grow in value and profitability in the months and years ahead? Are you a "growth stock," or has your value leveled off in the marketplace?

If you have decided to be a "growth stock," what is your strategy for increasing your income 25 percent to 30 percent every year, year after year? As the president of your own life, as the spouse or parent in your own family, you owe it to the important people in your life to be on a growth curve, to be continually increasing in value, income, and profitability as the years progress.

Take the Wheel of Your Own Life

From this point forward, see and think about yourself as the master of your own fate, as completely in charge of your own life. See yourself as the president of your own personal services corporation, a powerful person, completely self-determined and self-directed.

Refuse to whine and complain about events of the past, which cannot be changed. Instead, orient yourself toward the future and think of what you want and where you are going. Above all, think about your goals. The very act of thinking about your goals makes you positive and purposeful again.

Determine Your Locus of Control

A large body of psychological literature revolves around the Locus of Control Theory. In more than fifty years of research, psychologists have determined that your locus of control is the determining factor of your happiness or unhappiness in life. Here is why.

People with an *internal* locus of control feel that they are in complete control of their life. They feel strong, confident, and powerful. They are generally optimistic and positive. They feel terrific about themselves and very much in charge of their destiny.

On the other hand, people with an *external* locus of control feel controlled by external factors, by their boss, their bills, their marriage, their childhood problems, and their current situation. They feel out of control and as a result, they feel weak, angry, fearful, negative, hostile, and disempowered.

The good news is that there is a direct relationship between the amount of responsibility you accept and the amount of control you feel. The more you say, "I am responsible!" the more of an internal locus of control you develop and the more powerful and confident you feel.

The Golden Triangle

There is also a direct relationship between responsibility and happiness. The more responsibility you accept, the happier you become. It seems that all three—responsibility, control, and happiness—go together.

The more responsibility you accept, the greater amount of control you feel you have. The greater amount of control you feel you have, the happier and more confident you become. When you feel positive and in control of your life, you will set bigger and more challenging goals for yourself. You will also have the drive and determination to achieve them. You will feel as if you hold your life in your own hands and that you can make it into whatever you decide to.

It Is in Your Hands

The starting point of goal setting is for you to realize that you have virtually unlimited potential to be, have, or do anything you really want in life if you simply want it badly enough and are willing to work long enough and hard enough to achieve it.

The second part of goal setting is for you to accept complete responsibility for your life, and for everything that happens to you, with no blaming and no excuses.

With these two concepts clearly in mind—that you have unlimited potential and that you are completely responsible—you are now ready to move to the next step, which is to begin designing your ideal future.

▓ | TAKE CHARGE OF YOUR LIFE

1 Identify your biggest problem or source of negativity in life today. In what ways are you responsible for this situation?

2 See yourself as the president of your own company. How would you act differently if you owned 100 percent of the shares?

3 Resolve today to stop blaming anyone else for anything and instead accept complete responsibility in every area of your life. What actions should you be taking?

4 Stop making excuses and start making progress. Imagine that your favorite excuses have no basis in fact, and act accordingly.

5 See yourself as the primary creative force in your own life. You are where you are and what you are because of your own choices and decisions. What should you change?

6 Resolve today to forgive anyone who has ever hurt you in any way. Let it go. Refuse to discuss it again. Instead, get so busy working on something that is important to you that you don't have time to think about it again.

3

Create Your Own Future

*You will become as small as your controlling desire;
as great as your dominant aspiration.*

—JAMES ALLEN

In more than thirty-three hundred studies of leaders conducted over the years, there is a special quality that stands
out, one quality that all great leaders have in common. It is
the quality of *vision*. Leaders have vision. Nonleaders do not.

Earlier I said that the most important discovery in all of
human history is that you become what you think about
most of the time. What is it then that leaders think about most
of the time? And the answer is that leaders think about the
future and where they are going and what they can do to get
there.

Nonleaders, on the other hand, think about the present
and the pleasures and problems of the moment. They think
and worry about the past and what has happened that cannot be changed.

Think about the Future

We call this leadership quality "future orientation." Leaders
think about the future and what they want to accomplish and
where they want to arrive sometime down the road. Leaders

think about what they want and what can be done to achieve it. The good news is that when you begin to think about your future as well, you begin to think like a *leader*, and you will soon get the same results that leaders get.

Dr. Edward Banfield of Harvard concluded, after more than fifty years of research, that "long-time perspective" was the most important determinant of financial and personal success in life. Banfield defined long-time perspective as the "ability to think several years into the future while making decisions in the present." This is one of the most important discoveries ever made. Just think! The further you think into the future, the better decisions you will make in the present to assure that that future becomes a reality.

Become a Millionaire

For example, if you saved $100 per month from the age of twenty to the age of sixty-five, and you invested that money in a mutual fund earning an average of 10 percent per annum over time, you would be worth more than $1,118,000 when you retired.

Anyone who really wanted to could save $100 per month, if he or she had a long enough time perspective. What this means is that people starting work today can become millionaires over time if they begin early enough, save consistently enough, and hold to their long-term vision of financial independence.

Create a Five-Year Fantasy

In personal strategic planning, you should begin with a long-term view of your life, as well. You should begin by practicing *idealization* in everything you do. In the process of idealization, you create a *five-year fantasy* for yourself and begin thinking about what your life would look life in five years if it were perfect in every respect.

The biggest single obstacle to setting goals is "self-limiting beliefs." These involve areas where you believe yourself to be limited in some way. You may believe yourself to be inadequate or inferior in areas such as intelligence, ability, talent, creativity, personality, or something else. As a result, you sell yourself short. By underestimating yourself, you set either *no* goals or *low* goals that are far below what you are truly capable of accomplishing.

Imagine No Limitations

By combining *idealization* and *future orientation,* you cancel or neutralize this process of self-limitation. You imagine for the moment that you have *no limitations at all.* You imagine that you have all the time, talents, and abilities you could ever require to achieve any goal you could set for yourself. No matter where you are in life, you imagine that you have all the friends, contacts, and relationships you need to open every door and achieve anything you could really want. You imagine that you have no limitations whatsoever on what you could be, have, or do in the pursuit of the goals that are really important to you.

Practice Blue-Sky Thinking

In Charles Garfield's studies of "peak performers," he made an interesting discovery. He analyzed men and women who had achieved only average results at work for many years but who suddenly exploded into great success and accomplishment. He found that at the "take-off point" every one of them began engaging in what he called "blue-sky thinking."

In blue-sky thinking, you imagine that all things are possible for you, just like looking up into a clear blue sky, with no limits. You project forward several years and imagine that your life is perfect in every respect. You then look back to where you are today and ask yourself this question: What would have to have happened for me to have created my perfect future?

You then come back to where you are in the present in your own mind, and you ask, What would have to happen from this point forward for me to achieve all my goals sometime in the future?

Refuse to Compromise Your Dreams

When you practice idealization and future orientation, you make no compromises with your dreams and visions for yourself and your future. You don't settle for smaller goals or half successes. Instead, you "dream big dreams" and project forward mentally as though you are one of the most powerful people in the universe. You create your perfect future. You decide what you really want before you come back to the present moment and deal with what is possible for you within your current situation.

Start with your business and career. Imagine that your work life was perfect five years from now. Answer these questions:

1. What would it look like?
2. What would you be doing?
3. Where would you be doing it?
4. Who would you be working with? What level of responsibility would you have?
5. What kinds of skills and abilities would you have?

6. What kind of goals would you be accomplishing?

7. What level of status would you have in your field?

Practice No-Limit Thinking

When you answer these questions, imagine that you have no limits. Imagine that everything is possible for you. Peter Drucker once said, "We greatly overestimate what we can accomplish in one year. But we greatly underestimate what we can accomplish in five years." Don't let this happen to you.

Now, idealize your perfect financial life sometime in the future:

1. How much would you be earning five years from today?

2. What sort of lifestyle would you have?

3. What kind of home would you live in?

4. What kind of car would you drive?

5. What kind of material luxuries would you be providing for yourself and your family?

6. How much would you have in the bank?

7. How much would you be saving and investing each month and each year?

8. How much would you want to be worth when you retire?

Imagine that you have a Magic Slate. You can write down anything you want. You can erase anything that may have happened in the past and create whatever picture you desire for your future. You can clean the slate at any time and start over. You have no limits.

Imagine Your Perfect Family Life

Look at your family and relationships today and project five years into the future:

1. If your family life were perfect five years from now, what would it look like?
2. Who would you be with? Who would you *no longer* be with?
3. Where and how would you be living?
4. What kind of living standards would you have?
5. What kind of relationships would you have with the most important people in your life five years from now if everything were perfect in every respect?

When you fantasize and imagine your perfect future, the only question you ask is, *How?* This is the most powerful question of all. Asking it repeatedly stimulates your creativity and triggers ideas to help you accomplish your goals. Unsuccessful people always wonder whether or not a particular goal is possible. High achievers, on the other hand ask only the question, *"How?"* They then work to find ways to turn their visions and goals into realities.

Ideal Health and Fitness

Review your levels of health and fitness in every area:

1. If you were a perfect physical specimen five years from now, how would you look and feel?
2. What would be your ideal weight?
3. How much would you exercise each week?

4. What would be your overall level of health?

5. What changes would you have to start making today in your diet, exercise routines, and health habits to enjoy superb physical health sometime in the future?

You then imagine that you are an important and influential person, a "player" in your community. You are making a significant contribution to the world around you. You are making a difference with your life and in the lives of other people. If your social and community status and involvement were ideal,

1. What would you be doing?

2. What organizations would you be working with or contributing to?

3. What are the causes that you strongly believe in and support and how could you become more involved in those areas?

Just Do It!

The primary difference between high achievers and low achievers is "action orientation." Men and women who accomplish tremendous deeds in life are intensely action oriented. They are moving all the time. They are always busy. If they have an idea, they take action on it immediately.

On the other hand, low achievers and nonachievers are full of good intentions, but they always have an excuse for not taking action today. It is well said that "the road to hell is paved with good intentions."

Examine yourself in terms of your personal inventory of skills, knowledge, talent, education, and ability. If you were developed to the highest level possible for you (and there is virtually no limit), answer these questions:

1. What additional knowledge and skills would you have acquired five years from now?
2. In what areas would you be recognized as absolutely excellent in what you do?
3. What would you be doing each day in order to develop the knowledge and skills you need to be one of the top performers in your field sometime in the future?

Once you have answered these questions, the next question you ask is, How? How do you attain the skills and expertise you will require to lead your field in the years ahead?

Design Your Perfect Calendar

Decide how you would like to live your ideal lifestyle, day in and day out. Design your perfect calendar from January 1 to December 31:

1. What would you like to do on your weekends and vacations?
2. How much time would you like to take off each week, month, and year?
3. Where would you like to go?
4. How would you organize your year if you had no limitations and complete control over your time?

Proverbs 29:18 says, "Where there is no vision, the people perish." What this means is that if you lack an exciting vision for your future, you will "perish" inside in terms of lacking motivation and enthusiasm for what you are doing. But the reverse of this is that with an exciting future vision, you will be continuously motivated and stimulated every day to take the actions necessary to make your ideal vision a reality.

The Key to Happiness

You remember that "Happiness is the progressive realization of a worthy ideal." When you have clear, exciting goals and ideals, you will feel happier about yourself and your world. You will be more positive and optimistic. You will be more cheerful and enthusiastic. You will feel *internally* motivated to get up and get going every morning because every step you are taking will be moving you in the direction of something that is important to you.

Resolve to think about your ideal future most of the time. Remember, the very best days of your life lie ahead. The happiest moments you will ever experience are still to come. The highest income you will ever earn is going to materialize in the months and years ahead. The future is going to be better than anything that may have happened in your past. There are no limits.

The clearer you can be about your long-term future, the more rapidly you will attract people and circumstances into your life to help make that future a reality. The greater clarity you have about who you are and what you want, the more you will achieve and the faster you will achieve it in every area of your life.

▓ | CREATE YOUR OWN FUTURE

1 Imagine that there is a solution to every problem, a way to overcome every limitation, and no limit on your achieving every goal you can set for yourself. What would you do differently?

2 Practice "back from the future thinking." Project forward five years and look back to the present. What would have to have happened for your world to be ideal?

3 Imagine your financial life was perfect in every way. How much would you be earning? How much would you be worth? What steps could you take, starting today, to make these goals a reality?

4 Imagine your family and personal life was perfect. What would it look like? What should you start doing more of, or less of, starting today?

5 Plan your perfect calendar. Design your year from January to December as if you had no limitations. What would you change, starting today?

6 Imagine that your levels of health and fitness were perfect in every way. What could you do, starting today, to make your vision for yourself into a reality?

4

Clarify Your Values

*One universe made up of all that is: and one God
in it all, and one principle of being, and one law, the
reason shared by all thinking creatures, and one truth.*

—MARCUS AURELIUS

One of the most important characteristics of leaders, and the most successful people in every area of life, is that they know *who* they are, what they believe in, and what they stand for. Most people are confused about their goals, values, and ideals, and as a result, they go back and forth and accomplish very little. Men and women who become leaders, on the other hand, with the same or even fewer abilities and opportunities, go on to great accomplishments in whatever they attempt.

Life is lived from the inside out. The very core of your personality is your *values*. Your values are what make you the person you are. Everything you do on the outside is dictated and determined by your values on the inside, whether clear or fuzzy. The greater clarity you have regarding your values on the inside, the more precise and effective will be your actions on the outside.

The Five Levels of Personality

You can imagine your personality by thinking of a target with concentric rings. Your personality is made up of five rings, starting from the center with your values and radiating outward to the next circle, your beliefs.

Your values determine your beliefs, about yourself and the world around you. If you have positive values, such as love, compassion, and generosity, you will believe that people in your world are deserving of these values and you will treat them accordingly.

Your beliefs, in turn, determine the third ring of your personality, *your expectations.* If you have positive values, you will believe yourself to be a good person. If you believe yourself to be a good person, you will expect good things to happen to you. If you expect good things to happen to you, you will be positive, cheerful, and future oriented. You will look for the good in other people and situations.

The fourth level of your personality, determined by your expectations, is your *attitude.* Your attitude will be an outward manifestation or reflection of your values, beliefs, and expectations. For example, if your value is that this is a good world to live in and your belief is that you are going to be very successful in life, you will expect that everything that happens to you is helping you in some way. As a result, you will have a positive mental attitude toward other people and they will respond positively toward you. You will be a more cheerful and optimistic person. You will be someone who others want to work with and for, buy from and sell to, and generally help to be more successful. This is why a positive mental attitude seems to go hand in hand with great success in every walk of life.

The fifth ring, or level of life, is your *actions.* Your actions on the outside will ultimately be a reflection of your innermost values, beliefs, and expectations on the inside. This is why what you achieve in life and work will be determined more by what is going on inside of you than by any other factor.

As Within, So Without

You can tell how people think, most of the time, by looking at the conditions of their outer lives. A positive, optimistic, goal- and future-oriented person—on the inside—will enjoy a happy, successful, and prosperous life on the outside, most of the time.

Aristotle said that the ultimate aim or purpose of human life is to achieve your own happiness. You are the very happiest when what you are doing on the outside is *congruent* with your values on the inside. When you are living in complete alignment with what you consider to be good and right and true, you will automatically feel happy and positive about yourself and your world.

Your goals must be congruent with your values, and your values must be congruent with your goals. This is why clarifying your values is often the starting point to high achievement and peak performance. Values clarification requires that you think through what is really important to you in life. You then organize your entire life around these values.

Any attempt to live on the outside in a manner that contradicts the values you hold on the inside will cause you stress, negativity, unhappiness, pessimism, and even anger and frustration. Your chief responsibility to yourself in the creation of a great life is therefore for you to develop absolute clarity about your values in everything you do.

Know What You Really Want

Stephen Covey once said, "Be sure that, as you scramble up the ladder of success, it is leaning against the right building." Many people work hard to achieve goals that they think they want only to find, at the end of the day, that they get no joy or satisfaction from their accomplishments. They ask, "Is this all there is?" This occurs when the outer accomplishment is not in harmony with your inner values. Don't let this happen to you.

Socrates said, "The unexamined life is not worth living." This applies to your values as much as to any other area of your life. Values clarification is something you do on a "go-forward" basis. You continually stop the clock, like a time-out in a football game, and ask, "What are my values in this area?"

In Matthew 16:26, the Bible says, *"What is a man profited if he shall gain the whole world, and lose his own soul?"* The happiest people in the world today are those who are living in harmony with their innermost convictions and values. The unhappiest people are those who are attempting to live incongruent with what they truly value and believe.

Trust Your Intuition

Self-trust is the foundation of greatness. Self-trust comes from listening to your intuition, to your "still, small voice" within. Men and women begin to become great when they begin to listen to their inner voices and absolutely trust that they are being guided by a higher power each step of the way.

Living in alignment with your true values is the royal road to self-confidence, self-respect, and personal pride. In fact, almost every human problem can be resolved by returning to values. Whenever you experience stress of any kind, look into yourself and ask, "In what way am I compromising my innermost values in this situation?"

Watch Your Behavior

How can you tell what your values really are? The answer is simple. You always demonstrate your true values in your *actions* and especially your actions *under pressure.* Whenever you are forced to choose between one behavior and another, you will always act consistent with what is most important and valuable to you at that moment.

Values, in fact, are organized in a hierarchy. You have a series of values, some of them very intense and important and some of them weaker and less important. One of the most important exercises you can engage in to determine *who* you really are and *what* you really want is to organize your values by priority. Once you are clear about the relative importance of your values, you can then organize your outer life so that it is in alignment with them.

Examine Your Past Behavior

There are some insightful ways to help you determine your true values. First of all, you can look at your past. How have you behaved under pressure in the past? What choices did you make with your time or money when you were forced to choose? Your answers will give you an indication of your predominant values at that time.

Dale Carnegie once wrote, *"Tell me what gives a person his greatest feeling of importance, and I will tell you his entire philosophy of life."* What makes you feel important? What raises your self-esteem? What increases your sense of self-respect and personal pride? What have you accomplished in your past life that has given you the greatest sense of pride and satisfaction? These answers will give you good indications of your true values.

Determine Your Heart's Desire

The spiritual teacher Emmet Fox wrote about the importance of discovering your *"heart's desire."* What is your heart's desire? What is it that, deep down in your heart, more than anything else, you would like to be, have, or do in life? As a friend of mine asks, "What do you want to be famous for?"

What words would you like people to use to describe you when you are not there? What would you like someone to say about you at your funeral? How would you want your family, friends, and children to remember you? How would you like people to talk to them about you?

What kind of a reputation do you have today? What kind of a reputation would you like to have sometime in the future? What would you have to begin doing today in order to create the kind of reputation that you desire?

Your Past Is Not Your Future

Many people had difficult experiences growing up. They fell on hard times and became associated with the wrong people. They had behaved in ways that were illegal or socially unacceptable. Some were even convicted and sent to prison for their crimes. But at a certain point in life, they decided to change. They thought seriously about the kind of person that they wanted to be known as, and thought of, in the future. They decided to change their lives by changing the values that they lived by. By making these decisions and sticking to them, they changed their lives. And what others have done, you can do as well.

Remember: **It doesn't matter where you're coming from; all that really matters is where you're going.**

If you were an outstanding person in every respect, how would you behave toward others? What sort of impression would you leave on others after you had met them and spoken with them? Imagine you could be a completely excellent person. How would you be different from who you are today?

How Much You Like Yourself

In psychology, your level of self-esteem determines your level of happiness. Self-esteem is defined as "how much you like yourself." Your self-esteem, in turn, is determined by your *self-image*. This is the way you see yourself and think about yourself in your day-to-day interactions with others. Your self-image is shaped by your self-ideal. Your self-ideal is made up of your virtues, values, goals, hopes, dreams, and aspirations.

Here is what psychologists have discovered: the more your behavior in the moment is consistent with what you feel your *ideal* behavior should be, the more you like and respect yourself and the happier you are.

On the other hand, whenever you behave in a way that is *inconsistent* with your ideal of your very best behavior, you experience a negative self-image. You feel yourself to be performing below your best, below what you truly aspire to. As a result, your self-esteem and your level of happiness decrease.

Perform at Your Best

The moment that you begin walking, talking, and behaving in ways that are consistent with your highest ideals, your self-image improves, your self-esteem increases, and you feel happier about yourself and your world.

For example, whenever you are complimented or praised by another person or given a prize or an award for accomplishment, your self-esteem goes up, sometimes dramatically. You feel happy about yourself. You feel that your whole life is in harmony and that you are living congruent with your highest ideals. You feel successful and valuable.

Your aim should be to deliberately and systematically create the circumstances that raise your self-esteem in everything you do. You should live your life as if you were already the outstanding person that you intend to be sometime in the future.

Know What You Believe

What are your values today with regard to your *work* and your *career?* Do you believe in the values of integrity, hard work, dependability, creativity, cooperation, initiative, ambition, and getting along well with people? People who live these values in their work are vastly more successful and more highly esteemed than people who do not.

What are your values with regard to your *family?* Do you believe in the importance of unconditional love, continuous encouragement and reinforcement, patience, forgiveness, generosity, warmth, and attentiveness? People who practice these values consistently with the important people in their lives are much happier than people who do not.

What are your values with regard to *money* and *financial success?* Do you believe in the importance of honesty, industry, thrift, frugality, education, excellent performance, quality, and persistence? People who practice these values are far more successful in their financial lives than those who do not, and they achieve their financial goals far faster as well.

What about your health? Do you believe in the importance of self-discipline, self-mastery, and self-control with regard to diet, exercise, and rest? Do you set high standards for health and fitness and then work every day to live up to those standards? People who practice these values live longer, healthier lives than people who do not.

Think Only about What You Want

Remember, you become what you think about most of the time. Successful, happy people think about their values and how they can live and practice those values in every part of their lives every single day. The big payoff is that the more you live your life consistent with your values, the happier, healthier, more positive and energetic you will be.

Be True to Yourself

Perhaps the most important value of all is that of *integrity*. A billionaire once said to me, "Integrity is not so much a value in itself; it is rather the value that guarantees all the other values."

This was a great insight for me! Once you have decided that you are going to live consistent with a value, your level of integrity determines whether or not you follow through on your commitment. The more you discipline yourself to live consistent with the very best you know, the greater is your level of personal integrity. And the higher your level of integrity, the happier and more powerful you will feel in everything you do.

Truly great men and women are always described as having high levels of integrity. They live their lives consistent with their highest values, even when no one is looking. Mediocre men and women, on the other hand, are always cutting corners and compromising their integrity, especially when no one is watching.

Live in Truth with Yourself and Others

Decide today to be a man or woman of *honor.* Resolve to tell the truth and to live in truth with yourself and others.

Crystallize your values in each area of your life. Write them down. Think of how you would behave if you were living consistent with those values, and then refuse to compromise them for any reason.

Once you accept complete responsibility for your life and for everything that happens to you and then create an ideal picture of your perfect future and clarify your values, you are ready to begin setting clear, specific goals in every area of your life. You are now on the launching ramp and ready to take off toward the stars.

⚏ CLARIFY YOUR VALUES

1 Make a list of your three to five most important values in life today. What do you really believe in and stand for?

2 What qualities and values are you best known for today among the people who know you?

3 What do you consider to be the most important values guiding your relationships with others in your life?

4 What are your values regarding money and financial success? Are you practicing these values daily?

5 Describe your picture of an ideal person, the person you would most want to be if you had no limitations.

6 Write your own obituary to be read to your friends and family at your funeral, exactly as you would like to be remembered.

7 What one change could you make in your behavior today that would help you to live in greater harmony with your values?

5

Determine Your True Goals

*Realize what you really want. It stops you from
chasing butterflies and puts you to work digging gold.*

—WILLIAM MOULTON MARSDEN

My favorite word in goal setting, and in success in general, is "clarity." There is a direct relationship between the level of clarity you have about who you are and what you want and virtually everything you accomplish in life.

Successful men and women invest the time necessary to develop absolute clarity about themselves and what they really want, like designing a detailed blueprint for a building before they begin construction. Most people just throw themselves at life like a dog chasing a passing car and wonder why they never seem to catch anything or keep anything worthwhile.

Henry David Thoreau once wrote, "Have you built your castles in the air? Good. That is where they should be built. Now, go to work and build foundations under them."

In this chapter, you will begin to crystallize your visions and values into concrete goals and objectives that you can work on every single day.

Make Your Goals Personal

Earlier I mentioned that intense, burning desire is absolutely essential to overcoming obstacles and achieving great goals.

For your desire to be intense enough, your goals must be purely personal. They must be goals that you choose for yourself rather than goals that someone else wants for you or that you want to achieve to please someone in your life. In goal setting, for the process to be effective you must be perfectly selfish about what you *really* want for yourself.

This doesn't mean that you cannot do things for other people either at home or at work. This simply means that in setting goals for your life, you start with yourself and work forward.

The Great Question

One of the most important questions in goal setting is this: **What do I really want to do with my life?** If you could do or be or have anything at all in life, what would it be? Remember, you can't hit a target you can't see. You should return to this question over and over again in the months and years ahead.

In determining your true goals, you start with your vision, your values, and your ideals. When you begin, these will often feel a bit like fantasies, detached from reality. However, now your job is to make them concrete, like designing a dream house on paper.

Decide What You *Really* Want

You start with your general goals and then move to more specific goals:

1. What are your three most important goals in your business and career right now?

2. What are your three most important financial goals right now?

3. What are your three most important family or relationship goals right now?

4. What are your three most important health and fitness goals right now?

Identify Your Major Worries

The flip side of the above questions is this: **What are my three biggest worries or concerns in life right now?** What bothers you, worries you, concerns you, and preoccupies you in your day-to-day life? What aggravates or irritates you? What is robbing you of happiness, more than anything else? As a friend of mine often asks, "Where does it hurt?"

Once you have identified your biggest problems, worries, or concerns, ask yourself,

1. What are the ideal solutions to each of these problems?

2. How could I eliminate these problems or worries immediately?

3. What is the fastest and most direct way to solve each problem?

A Great Thinking Tool

In 1142, William of Ockham, a British philosopher, proposed a method of problem solving that has come to be referred to as "Ockham's razor." This way of thinking has become famous and popular throughout the ages. Ockham said, "The simplest and most direct solution, requiring the fewest number of steps, is usually the correct solution to any problem."

Many people make the mistake of overcomplicating goals and problems. But the more complicated the solution, the less likely it is ever to be implemented and the longer the time it will take to get any results. Your aim should be to simplify the solution and go directly to the goal as quickly as possible.

Double Your Income

Many people tell me that they would like to double their incomes. If they are in sales, I ask them, "What is the fastest and most direct way to double your income?" After they have come up with a series of suggestions, I give them what I consider to be the best answer: "Double the amount of time that you spend face to face with qualified prospects."

The most direct way to increase your sales has always been the same: Spend more time with better prospects. If you don't upgrade your skills or change anything else about what you are doing but you double the number of *minutes* that you spend face to face with prospects each day, you will probably double your sales income.

According to studies that go back as far as 1928, on average salespeople today spend ninety minutes each day face to face with prospects. The highest paid salespeople spend two or three times that amount. They organize their days efficiently to assure that they spend more minutes in the presence of people who can and will buy their products or services. And the more time they spend with prospects and customers, the more skilled they become at selling. The better they get, the more they sell and the more they earn in less time.

Double Your Productivity

If you examined your work, you would find that 20 percent of what you do accounts for 80 percent of what you do. In my Advanced Coaching Programs, we teach our clients to identify those 20 percent of activities that contribute the most value and then do *twice* as many of them.

Instead of using their intelligence to juggle their time and accomplish a greater number of tasks, we teach them to do fewer tasks but tasks of higher value. Some of our clients double their productivity and subsequently their income in as little as thirty days with this approach, even if they have been working for many years in the same position.

Always look for the simplest and most direct way to get from where you are to where you want to go. Look for the solution that has the fewest number of steps. And most of all, take action! Get going. Get busy. Develop a "sense of urgency." The best ideas in the world are of no value until they are implemented. As the poet John Greenleaf Whittier said, "Of all the sad words of tongue and pen, the saddest are these: it might have been."

Wave a Magic Wand

In determining your true goals, use the "magic wand" technique. Imagine that you have a magic wand that you can wave over a particular area of your life. When you wave this magic wand, your wishes come true!

Wave a magic wand over your business and career. If you could have any three wishes in your work, what would they be? Wave a magic wand over your financial life. If you could have any three wishes in your financial life, what would they be?

Wave a magic wand over your family life and your relationships. If you could have any three wishes in this area, what would they be? If your family life were ideal in every respect, what would it look like?

Wave a magic wand over your health and fitness. If you could have any three wishes with regard to your body and your physical well-being, what would they be? If your health were perfect, how would it be different from today?

Wave a magic wand over your skills and abilities. If you could have any three skills or abilities, developed to a high level, what would they be? In what areas would you like to excel?

The magic wand technique is fun on the one hand, but quite revealing on the other. Whenever you imagine that you have a magic wand, your true goals in that area emerge. You can also use this exercise for other people who are not sure about what they want or where they are going. It is amazing what comes out when you ask this question.

Six Months to Live

Here is another goal-setting question that reflects your true values. Imagine that you go to a doctor for a full medical check-up. Your doctor calls you back a few days later and says, "I have good news for you and I have bad news for you. The good news is that for the next six months you are going to live the healthiest and most energetic life you could possibly imagine. The bad news is that at the end of 180 days, because of an incurable illness, you will drop dead."

If you learned today that you had only six months left to live, how would you spend your last six months on earth? Who would you spend the time with? Where would you go? What would you strive to complete? What would you do more of or less of?

When you ask yourself this question, what comes to the top of your mind will be a reflection of your true values. Your answer will almost always include the most important people in your life. Very few people in this situation would say, "Well, I'd like to get back to the office and return a few phone calls."

Make Up Your Dream List

In setting your true goals as an extension of imagining that you have no limitations, make up a *dream list*. A dream list is a list of everything you would like to be, have, or do sometime in your life if you had no limitations at all.

Mark Victor Hansen, coauthor of *Chicken Soup for the Soul,* recommends that you sit down with a pad of paper and make a list of at least one hundred goals that you want to accomplish in your lifetime. Then imagine that you have all the time, money, friends, abilities, and resources necessary to achieve these goals. Let yourself dream and fantasize. Just write down everything that you would like to have as if you had no limitations at all.

The amazing discovery you will make is that within thirty days after writing out this list of one hundred dreams, remarkable events will begin to happen in your life and your goals will start to be achieved at a rate that you cannot even imagine today. This seems to happen to virtually all people once they have written down at least one hundred goals. You should give it a try. You could be amazed at the results.

The Instant Millionaire

Here is another goal-setting question: **If you won a million dollars cash tomorrow, tax free, how would you change your life?** What would you do differently? What would you get into or out of? What would you do more of or less of? What would be the first thing you would do?

This is a way of asking the question, How would you change your life if you were completely *free to choose*? The primary reason that we stay in situations that are not the best for us is because we fear change. But when you imagine that you have all the money that you will ever need, to do or be whatever you want, your true goals often emerge.

For example, if you were currently in the wrong job for you, the idea of winning a large amount of money would cause you to think about quitting that job immediately. If you were in the right job for you, however, winning a lot of money would not affect your career choice at all. So ask yourself, What would I do if I won a million dollars cash, tax free, tomorrow?

No Fear of Failure

Here is another question to help you clarify your true goals: **What have you always wanted to do but been afraid to attempt?** When you look around your world and you see other people who are doing things that you admire, which of these have you always wanted to do as well?

Have you wanted to start your own business? Have you wanted to run for public office? Have you wanted to embark on a new career? What have you always wanted to do but been afraid to attempt?

Do What You Love to Do

In setting goals for your life, short and long-term, you should continually ask yourself, **What do I most enjoy doing in each area of my life?** For instance, if you could do just one thing all day long in your work, what would it be? If you could do any job or full-time activity all the time, without pay, what would it be? What sort of work or activity gives you the greatest joy and satisfaction?

The psychologist Abraham Maslow identified what he called "peak experiences," those moments or times when an individual feels the happiest, most elated, and most exhilarated. One of your aims in life is to enjoy as many peak experiences as possible. You achieve this by thinking back and identifying those moments of peak experience in your past and then by imagining how you could repeat them in your present and future. What have been your happiest moments in life up to now? How could you have more of those moments in the future? *What do you really love to do?*

Make a Difference

You should have goals for social and community involvement and contribution as well. **What kind of difference would you like to make in your world?** What organizations, causes, needs, or social problems would you like to work on or in? What changes would you like to see? Who is there who is less fortunate than you that you would like to help?

If you were independently wealthy, what causes would you support? Most of all, what could you do today to begin making a difference in your world? Don't wait until some future date when everything will be ideal. Instead, start today in some way.

Set Clear Financial Goals

One of the most important areas of goal setting is your financial life. If you could earn and accumulate all the money you need, you could probably achieve most of your nonfinancial goals faster and easier.

If your life were ideal, how much money would you like to earn each month, each year? How much would you like to save and invest each month and year? How much would you like to be worth sometime in the future? What sort of estate would you like to accumulate by the time you retire and when would you like that to be? Most people are hopelessly confused about their financial goals, but when you become absolutely clear about them for yourself, your ability to achieve them increases dramatically.

Clarity Makes Your Dreams Become Your Realities

When you are absolutely clear about what you want, you can then think about your goals most of the time. And the more you think about them, the faster they will materialize in your life.

This process of asking yourself questions about your goals in each part of your life begins to clarify your thinking and make you a more focused and better-defined person. As Zig Ziglar says, "You move from being a wandering generality to becoming a meaningful specific."

Most of all, you reach the point where you can determine your major definite purpose in life. This is the springboard for great achievement and extraordinary accomplishment.

Your major definite purpose will be the topic of the next chapter, and how to achieve it will be the subject of the chapters to come.

▓ DETERMINE YOUR TRUE GOALS

1 Write down your three most important goals in life right now.

2 What are your three most pressing problems or worries right now?

3 If you won a million dollars cash, tax free, tomorrow, what changes in your life would you make immediately?

4 What do you really love to do? What gives you the greatest feelings of value, importance, and satisfaction?

5 If you could wave a magic wand over your life and have anything you wanted, what would you wish for?

6 What would you do, how would you spend your time, if you had only six months left to live?

7 What would you really want to do with your life if you had no limitations?

6

Decide upon Your Major Definite Purpose

There is one quality which one must possess to win,
and that is definiteness of purpose, the knowledge
of what one wants, and a burning desire to possess it.

—NAPOLEON HILL

Since you become what you think about most of the time, a major definite purpose gives you a focus for every waking moment. As Peter Drucker said, "Whenever you find something getting done, you find a monomaniac with a mission."

The more you think about your major definite purpose and how to achieve it, the more you activate the Law of Attraction in your life. You begin to attract people, opportunities, ideas, and resources that help you to move more rapidly toward your goal and move your goal more rapidly toward you.

By the Law of Correspondence, your outer world of experience will correspond and harmonize with your inner world of goals. When you have a major definite purpose that you think about, talk about, and work on all the time, your outer world will reflect this, like a mirror image.

A major definite purpose also activates your subconscious mind on your behalf. Any thought, plan, or goal that you can clearly define in your conscious mind will immediately start to be brought into reality by your subconscious mind (and your superconscious mind, as we will discuss later).

Activate Your Reticular Cortex

Each person has within his or her brain a special organ called the "reticular cortex." This small, finger-like part of the brain functions in a way similar to a telephone switchboard in a large office building. Just as all phone calls are received by the central switchboard and then rerouted to the appropriate recipient, all incoming information to your senses is routed through your reticular cortex to the relevant part of your brain or your awareness.

Your reticular cortex contains your *reticular activating system.* When you send a goal message to your reticular cortex, it starts to make you intensely aware of and alert to people, information, and opportunities in your environment that will help you to achieve your goal.

A Red Sports Car

For example, imagine that you decided that you wanted a red sports car. You write this down as a goal. You begin to think about and visualize a red sports car. This process sends the message to your reticular cortex that a red sports car is now important to you. A picture of a red sports car immediately goes up onto your mental radar screen.

From that moment onward, you will start to notice red sports cars wherever you go. You will even see them driving and turning corners several blocks away. You will see them parked in driveways and in showrooms. Everywhere you go, your world will seem to be full of red sports cars.

If you decided to buy a motorcycle, you would start to see motorcycles everywhere. If you decided to take a trip to

Hawaii, you would begin to notice posters, advertisements, brochures, and television specials with information on Hawaiian vacations. Whatever goal message you send to your reticular cortex causes your reticular activating system to make you alert to all possible ways to make that goal a reality.

Achieve Financial Independence

If you decide to become financially independent, you will suddenly begin to notice all kinds of opportunities and possibilities around you that have to do with achieving your financial goals. You will see stories in newspapers and recognize books on the subject wherever you go. You will receive information and solicitations in the mail. You will find yourself in conversations about earning and investing money. It will seem as though you are surrounded by ideas and information that can be helpful to you in achieving your financial goals.

On the other hand, if you do not give clear instructions to your reticular cortex and your subconscious mind, you will go through life as though you were driving in a fog. You will be largely unaware of all these opportunities and possibilities around you. You will seldom see them or notice them.

It has been said "Attention is the key to life." Wherever your attention goes, your life goes as well. When you decide upon a major definite purpose, you increase your level of attentiveness and become increasingly sensitive to anything in your environment that can help you to achieve that goal faster.

Your Major Definite Purpose

Your major definite purpose can be defined as the one goal that is most important to you at the moment. It is usually the one goal that will help you to achieve more of your other goals than anything else you can accomplish. It must have the following characteristics:

1. It must be something that you *personally* really want. Your desire for this goal must be so intense that the very idea of achieving your major definite purpose excites you and makes you happy.

2. It must be clear and specific. You must be able to define it in words. You must be able to write it down with such clarity that a child could read it and know exactly what it is that you want and be able to determine whether or not you have achieved it.

3. It must be measurable and quantifiable. Rather than "I want to make a lot of money," it must be more like "I will earn $100,000 per year by (a specific date)."

4. It must be both believable and achievable. Your major definite purpose cannot be so big or so ridiculous that it is completely unattainable.

5. Your major definite purpose should have a reasonable probability of success, perhaps fifty-fifty when you begin. If you have never achieved a major goal before, set a goal that has an 80 percent or 90 percent probability of success. Make it easy on yourself, at least at the beginning. Later on, you can set huge goals with very small probabilities of success and you will still be motivated to take the steps necessary to achieve them. But in the beginning, set goals that are believable and achievable and that have a high probability of success so that you can be assured of *winning* right from the start.

6. Your major definite purpose must be in *harmony* with your other goals. You cannot want to be financially successful in your career on the one hand and play golf most of the time on the other. Your major goals must be in harmony with your minor goals and congruent with your values.

Keep Your Feet on the Ground

A woman approached me at one of my seminars and told me that she had decided upon her major definite purpose. I asked her what it was. She said, "I am going to be a millionaire in one year."

Curious I asked her approximately how much she was worth today. It turned out that she was broke. I asked her what kind of work she did. It turned out that she had just been fired from her job because of incompetence. I then asked her why she would set a goal to acquire a million dollars in one year under these circumstances.

She informed me that I had said that you could set any major goal you wanted as long as you were clear, and she was therefore convinced that was all she needed to be successful. I had to explain to her that her goal was so unrealistic and unattainable in her current circumstances that it would only discourage her when she found herself so far away from it. Such a goal would actually end up *demotivating* her rather than motivating her to do what she would need to do to be financially successful in the years ahead.

Be Honest with Yourself

A man at one of my seminars told me that his major definite purpose was "world peace." I explained to him that unless he was the head of a major superpower, there was very little influence he could have on world peace. Such a goal would only keep him from setting a personal goal that was attainable, something he could work on every day. He was visibly irritated and walked away, unhappy with my reluctance to encourage him in his fantasy.

In both of these cases, people were using goal setting *against* themselves. They were setting themselves up for failure by creating goals that were so unachievable that they would soon become discouraged and quit making any efforts at all.

This is a real danger when you begin setting big goals for yourself, and you must be careful to avoid it. It can be a blind alley that leads you into discouragement and demotivation rather than to enthusiasm and excitement.

Don't Sabotage Yourself

I made this same mistake myself when I was younger. When I first started setting goals, I set an income goal that was ten times what I had ever earned in my life. After many months and no progress at all, I realized that my goal was not helping me. Because it was so far beyond anything that I had ever achieved, it had no motivating power. In my heart of hearts, although I wanted it I really did not *believe* it was possible. And since I did not believe it was possible, my subconscious mind rejected it and my reticular cortex simply failed to function. Don't let this happen to you.

The Great Question

Here is the key question for determining your major definite purpose: **What one great thing would you dare to dream if you knew you could not fail?**

If you could be absolutely guaranteed of successfully achieving any goal, large or small, short term or long term, what one goal would it be? Whatever your answer to this question, if you can write it down, you can probably achieve it. From then on, the only question you should ask is, *How?* The only real limit is how badly you want it and how long you are willing to work toward it.

A Nobel Prize Winner

One of my seminar participants, a professor of chemistry at a leading university, had won a Nobel Prize in chemistry two years before in partnership with two other scientists. He told me that when he started his university career in his twenties, he decided that he wanted to make a major contribution in the field of chemistry. That was his major definite purpose. He focused on it for more than 25 years. And eventually he was successful.

He told me, "I was clear from the very beginning. I never doubted that I would eventually make such a significant contribution to chemistry that I would win the Nobel Prize. I was happy when it happened, but it was not a surprise."

Be Willing to Pay the Price

Everyone wants to be a millionaire or a multimillionaire. The only question is whether or not you are willing to do everything necessary and invest all the years required to achieve that financial goal. If you are, there is virtually nothing that can stop you.

The Ten-Goal Exercise

Here is an exercise for you. Take out a sheet of paper and write down a list of ten goals you would like to accomplish in the foreseeable future. Write them in the present tense, as though you had already achieved these goals. For example, you would write, "I weigh XXX pounds." Or, "I earn XXX dollars per year."

After you have completed your list of ten goals, go back over the list and ask yourself this question: What one goal on this list, if I were to accomplish it immediately, would have the greatest positive impact on my life?

In almost every case, this one goal is your major definite purpose. It is the one goal that can have the greatest impact on your life and on the achieving of most of your other goals at the same time.

Whatever goal you choose, write it on a separate sheet of paper. Write down everything that you can think of that you can do to achieve this goal, and then take action on at least one item on your list. Write this goal on a three-inch by five-inch index card that you carry around with you and review regularly. Think about this goal morning, noon, and night. Continually look for ways to achieve it. And the only question you should ask is, *How?*

Think about Your Goal

Your selection of a major definite purpose and your decision to concentrate single-mindedly on that purpose, overcoming all obstacles and difficulties until it is achieved, will do more to change your life for the better than any other decision you ever make. Whatever your major definite purpose, write it down and begin working on it today.

⚙ | DECIDE UPON YOUR MAJOR DEFINITE PURPOSE

1 What one great thing would you dare to dream if you knew you could not fail?

2 Make a list of ten goals you would like to achieve in the months and years ahead, in the present tense. Select the one goal from that list that would have the greatest positive impact on your life.

3 Determine how you will measure progress and success in the achieving of this goal. Write it down.

4 Make a list of everything you can do that will move you toward your goal. Take action on at least one thing immediately.

5 Determine the price you will have to pay in additional work, time, and commitment to achieve your goal, and then get busy paying that price.

7

Analyze Your Beliefs

The only thing that stands between a man and
what he wants from life is often merely the will
to try it and the faith to believe that it is possible.

—RICHARD M. DEVOS

Perhaps the most important of all mental laws is the Law
of Belief. This law says that **whatever you believe with conviction becomes your reality.** You do not believe what you
see; you see what you already believe. You actually view your
world through a lens of beliefs, attitudes, prejudices, and pre-
conceived notions. You are not what you think you are, but
what you think, you are.

Proverbs 23:7 says that as a man *"thinketh in his heart, so
is he."* This means that you always act on the outside based
on your innermost beliefs and convictions about yourself.

In Matthew 9:29, Jesus says "According to your faith, [it
will be done] unto you." This is another way of saying that
your intense beliefs become your realities. They determine
what happens to you.

Dr. William James of Harvard said in 1905, *"Belief cre-
ates the actual fact."* He went on to say, "The greatest revolution of my generation is the discovery that individuals, by
changing their inner attitudes of mind, can change the outer
aspects of their lives."

Change Your Thinking, Change Your Life

All improvement in your life comes from changing your beliefs about yourself and your possibilities. Personal growth comes from changing your beliefs about what you can do and about what is possible for you. Would you like to double your income? Of course you would! Here is the question: Do you believe that it is possible? How would you like to triple your income? Do you believe that is possible as well?

Whatever your level of skepticism, let me ask you a question. Since you started your first job, haven't you already doubled or tripled your income? Aren't you already earning vastly more than you earned when you started? Haven't you already proven to yourself that it is possible to double and triple your income? And what you have done before, you can do again—probably over and over—if you just learn how. You simply have to believe that it is possible.

Napoleon Hill said, "Whatever the mind of man can conceive and believe, it can achieve."

Your Master Program for Success

Perhaps the greatest breakthrough in the twentieth century in the field of human potential was the discovery of self-concept. Everything you do or achieve in your life, every thought, feeling, or action, is controlled and determined by your self-concept. **Your self-concept precedes and predicts your levels of performance and effectiveness in everything you do.** Your self-concept is the master program of your mental computer. It is the basic operating system. Everything that you accomplish in your outer world is a result of your self-concept.

What psychologists have discovered is that your self-concept is made up of the sum total of all of your beliefs, attitudes, feelings, and opinions about yourself and your world. Because of this, you always operate in a manner consistent with your self-concept, whether positive or negative.

Garbage in, Garbage Out

Here is an interesting discovery about self-concept. Even if your self-concept is made up of *erroneous* beliefs about yourself or your world, as far as you are concerned these are facts and you will think, feel, and act accordingly.

As it happens, your beliefs about yourself are largely *subjective*. They are often not based on fact at all. They are the result of information you have taken in throughout your life and the way you have processed that information. Your beliefs have been shaped and formed by your early childhood, your friends and associates, your reading and education, your experiences—both positive and negative—and a thousand other factors.

The worst of all beliefs are *self-limiting beliefs*. If you believe yourself to be limited in some way, whether or not it is true, it becomes true for you. If you believe it, you will act as if you were deficient in that particular area of talent or skill. Overcoming self-limiting beliefs and self-imposed limitations is often the biggest obstacle standing between you and the realization of your full potential.

Ignore the Experts

Albert Einstein was sent home from school as a young man with a learning disability. His parents were told that he was incapable of being educated. They refused to accept this diagnosis and eventually arranged for him to get an excellent education.

Dr. Albert Schweitzer had the same problems at school as a boy. His parents were encouraged to apprentice him to a shoemaker so that he would have a safe, secure job when he grew up. Both men went on to earn doctorates before the age of twenty and to leave their marks on the history of the twentieth century.

According to an article in *Fortune* magazine on learning disabilities in business, many presidents and senior executives of Fortune 500 corporations today were diagnosed in school as being not particularly bright or capable. But by virtue of hard work, they went on to achieve great success in their industries.

Thomas Edison was expelled from school in the sixth grade. His parents were told that it would be a waste of time to spend any money educating him because he was not particularly smart or capable of being taught anything. Edison went on to become the greatest inventor of the modern age. This kind of story has been repeated thousands of times.

Self-limiting beliefs, sometimes based on a single experience or a casual remark, can hold you back for years. Most people have had the experience of mastering a skill in an area where they thought they had no ability and being quite surprised at themselves. Perhaps this has happened to you. You suddenly realize that your limiting ideas about yourself in that area were not based on fact at all.

You Are Better Than You Know

Louise Hay, the writer, says that the roots of most of our problems in life are contained in the feeling, "I'm not good enough." Dr. Alfred Adler said that it is the natural inheritance of Western man to have feelings of "inferiority" that start in childhood and often continue through adult life.

Many people, because of their negative beliefs, most of which are erroneous, *falsely* consider themselves to be limited in intelligence, talent, capability, creativity, or skill of some kind. In virtually every case, these beliefs are false.

The fact is that you have more potential than you could ever use in your entire lifetime. No one is better than you and no one is smarter than you. People are just smarter or better in different areas at different times.

You Could Be a Genius

According to Dr. Howard Gardner of Harvard University, the founder of the concept of multiple intelligences, you possess at least ten different intelligences, in any one of which you might be a genius.

Unfortunately, only two intelligences are measured and reported throughout school and university: verbal and mathematical. But you could be a genius in the areas of *visio-spatial* intelligence (art, design), *entrepreneurial* intelligence (business start-ups), *physical* or *kinesthetic* intelligence (sports), *musical* intelligence (playing musical instruments, writing music), *interpersonal* intelligence (getting along well with others), *intrapersonal* intelligence (understanding yourself at a deep level), *intuitive* intelligence (ability to sense the right thing to do or say), *artistic* intelligence (creating works of art), or *abstract* intelligence (physics, science).

As the sign on the wall of an inner city school reads, "God don't make no junk." Each person is capable of achieving excellence in some way, in some area. You have within you, right now, the ability to function at genius or exceptional levels in at least one and perhaps several different intelligences. Your job is to find out which intelligence.

Your responsibility to yourself is to cast off all these self-limiting beliefs and accept that you are an extraordinarily capable and talented person. You are engineered for greatness and designed for success. You have competencies and capabilities that have never been tapped. You have the ability within yourself, right now, to accomplish almost any goal you can set for yourself if you are willing to work long enough and hard enough to achieve it.

Your Beliefs Are Acquired, Not Inborn

The good news about beliefs is that *all beliefs are learned.* They can therefore be unlearned, especially if they are not helpful. When you came into the world, you had no beliefs at all—about yourself, your religion, your political party, other people, or the world in general. Today, you "know" a lot of things. But, as the comic Josh Billings once wrote, "It ain't what a man knows what hurts him. It's what he knows what ain't true."

Many things that you *know* about yourself are simply not true. And these are almost always self-limiting beliefs. The starting point of unlocking more of your potential is for you to identify your self-limiting beliefs and then ask, "What if they were not true at all?"

What if you were possessed of an extraordinary ability in an area where you didn't think you were very good, such as selling, entrepreneurship, public speaking, or money making?

Think of Yourself Differently

Everywhere I go, throughout the world, I have taught these principles to tens of thousands of people. I have file drawers full of letters and e-mails from people who had never heard this idea of self-limiting beliefs before. But once they heard it, they changed their entire attitudes toward themselves. They began to see themselves as far more competent and capable in key areas of their lives than they had ever been before.

In no time at all, they began transforming their lives and changing their results. Their incomes doubled and tripled and quadrupled. Many of them became millionaires and multimillionaires. They went from the bottom of their companies to the top, from the worst performer in their sales forces to the highest earning person in their companies.

After they changed their beliefs about themselves and their personal potentials, they learned new skills and took on new challenges. They set bigger goals and threw their whole hearts into achieving them. By questioning their beliefs and by refusing to accept that they were limited in any way, they took complete charge of their lives and careers and created new realities for themselves. And what countless others have done, you can do as well.

Select the Beliefs You Want

Imagine that there was a "Belief Store," very much like a computer software store, where you could purchase a belief to program into your subconscious mind. If you could choose any set of beliefs at all, which beliefs would be the most helpful to you?

Here is my suggestion. Select this belief: **"I am destined to be a big success in life."**

If you absolutely *believe* that you are destined to be a big success, you will walk, talk, and act as if everything that happens to you in life is part of a great plan to make you successful. And as it happens, this is how the top people think in every field.

Look for the Good

Successful people look for the good in every situation. They know that it is always there. No matter how many reversals and setbacks they experience, they expect to get something good out of everything that happens to them. They *believe* that every setback is part of a great plan that is moving them inexorably toward achieving the great success that is inevitable for them.

If your beliefs are positive enough, you will seek the *valuable lesson* in every setback or difficulty. You will confidently believe that there are many lessons that you have to learn on the road to achieving and keeping your ultimate success. You therefore look upon every problem as a learning experience. Napoleon Hill wrote, "Within every difficulty or obstacle, there is the seed of an equal or greater advantage or benefit."

With this kind of an attitude, you benefit from everything that happens to you, positive or negative, as you move upward and onward toward achieving your major definite purpose.

Act Your Way into Feeling

The Law of Reversibility in psychology and metaphysics says, "You are more likely to act yourself into feeling a particular way than you are to feel yourself into acting."

What this means is that when you start, you may not feel like the great success that you desire to be. You will not have the self-confidence that comes from a record of successful achievement. You will often doubt your own abilities and fear failure. You will feel that you are not good enough, at least not yet.

But if you "act as if" you were already the person you desire to be, with the qualities and talents that you desire to have, your actions will generate the feelings that go with them. You will actually act yourself into feeling the way you want to feel by the Law of Reversibility.

If you want to be one of the top people in your business, dress like the top people. Groom yourself like the top people. Organize your work habits the way they do. Pick the most successful people in your field and use them as your role models. If possible, go to them and ask them for advice on how to get ahead more rapidly. And whatever advice they give you, follow it immediately. Take action.

When you start to walk, talk, dress, and behave like the top people, you soon begin to *feel* like the top people. You will treat other people like the top people do. You will work the way the top people work. You will start to get the results that the top people get. In no time at all, you will be one of the top people yourself. It may be trite to say "Fake it until you make it!" but there is a lot of truth to it.

The Secret of a Sales Manager

A friend of mine is a very successful sales manager. After he had carefully interviewed and then selected a new salesman, he would take the salesman to a Cadillac dealership and insist that he trade in his old car for a new Cadillac. The salesman would usually balk at the idea. He would be frightened of the cost of the car and the huge monthly payments involved. But the sales manager would insist that he buy the Cadillac as a condition of employment.

What do you think happened afterwards? First, the salesman would drive the car home and his wife would almost have a heart attack when she saw that he had bought a new Cadillac. But after she had settled down, he would take her for a ride around the neighborhood in the new car. The neighbors would see them driving in a new Cadillac as he waved on the way past. He would park his new Cadillac in front of his house or in his driveway. People would come over and admire it. Gradually, imperceptibly, at a subconscious level, his attitude toward himself and his earning potential would begin to change.

Within a few days, he would begin to see himself as the kind of person who drove a new Cadillac. He would see himself as a big money earner in his field, one of the top performers in his industry. And time after time, almost without fail, the salespeople in this organization became sales superstars. Their sales performance jumped and they earned more than they had ever before. Soon the payments on the new Cadillac were of no concern because their incomes were so much greater.

Create the Mental Equivalent

Emmet Fox, the spiritual teacher, once said, "Your main job in life is to create the mental equivalent within yourself of what you want to realize and enjoy in your outer world."

Your focus must be on creating the beliefs within yourself that are consistent with the great success you want to be in your outer world. You achieve this by challenging your self-limiting beliefs, rejecting them, and then acting as if they did not exist.

You reinforce the development of new, life-enhancing beliefs by increasing your knowledge and skills in your field to the point where you feel equal to any demand or challenge. You accelerate the development of new, positive beliefs by setting bigger and more exciting goals in every area. Finally, you act continually as if you were already the person that you desire to be.

Your aim is to reprogram your subconscious mind for success by creating the *mental equivalent* in everything you do or say.

Behave Consistent with Your New Self-Image

You develop new beliefs by taking actions consistent with those beliefs. You act as if you already believe that you have these capabilities and competences. You behave like a positive, optimistic, and cheerful person toward everyone. You act as if your success is already guaranteed. **You act as if you have a secret guarantee of success and only you know about it.**

You realize that you are developing, shaping, and controlling the evolution of your own character and personality by everything that you do and say every single day.

Since you become what you think about, you should only say and do what is consistent with your self-ideal, the person you most aspire to be, and your long-term future ideals. You should only think and talk about the qualities and behaviors that are moving you toward becoming the person you want to be and toward achieving the goals that you want to achieve.

Make a Decision

Make a decision this very day to challenge and reject any self-limiting beliefs that you might have that could be holding you back. Look into yourself and question the areas of your life where you have doubts about your abilities or talents. You might ask your friends and family members if they see any negative beliefs that you might have.

Often, they will be aware of self-limiting beliefs you have that you are not aware of yourself. In every case, once you have identified these negative beliefs, ask yourself, What if the opposite were true?

What if you had the ability to be extraordinarily successful in an area where you currently doubt yourself? What if you had been programmed from infancy with genius ability in a particular area? For example, what if you had within you, right now, the ability to earn and keep all the money you could ever want, throughout your life? What if you had a "golden touch" with regard to money?

If you absolutely believed these ideas to be true, what would you do differently from what you are doing today?

Keep Your Words and Actions Consistent

Your beliefs are always manifested in your words and actions. Make sure that everything you say and do from now on is consistent with the beliefs that you want to have and the person that you want to become. In time, you will replace more and more of your self-limiting beliefs with life-enhancing beliefs. Over time, you will completely reprogram yourself for success. When this occurs, the transformation that takes place in your outer life will amaze you and all the people around you.

▓ ANALYZE YOUR BELIEFS:

1 "Act as if!" If you were one of the most competent and highly respected people in your field, how would you think, act, and feel differently from today?

2 Imagine that you have a "golden touch" with money. If you were an extremely competent money manager, how would you handle your finances?

3 Identify the self-limiting beliefs that could be holding you back. How would you act if they were completely untrue?

4 Select a belief that you would most like to have about yourself at a deep inner level. Pretend as if you already believe this to be true about yourself.

5 Look into the most difficult situation you are dealing with right now. What valuable lessons does it contain that can help you to be better in the future?

8

Start at the Beginning

Your problem is to bridge the gap between where
you are now and the goals you intend to reach.

—EARL NIGHTINGALE

Imagine that you were going to take a long trip across the
country. The first step you would take would be to choose
your destination and then get a road map to determine the
very best way to get there. Each day before you started out,
you would locate yourself on a map relative to where you
were and where you planned to go in the hours ahead. Life is
very much the same.

Once you have decided upon your values, vision, mission, purpose, and goals, the next step is for you to analyze
your starting point. Exactly where are you today, and how
are you doing, in each of the important areas of your life,
especially as they relate to your goals?

Practice the Reality Principle

Jack Welch, CEO of General Electric for many years, once
said that the most important quality of leadership is the
"reality principle." He defined this as the ability to see the
world as it really is, not as you wish it were. He would begin

every meeting to discuss a goal or a problem with the question, "What's the reality?"

Peter Drucker refers to this quality as "intellectual honesty," dealing with the facts exactly as they are before attempting to solve a problem or make a decision. Abraham Maslow once wrote that the first quality of the self-actualizing person was the ability to be completely honest and objective with himself or herself. It is the same with you.

If you want to be the best you can be and achieve what is truly possible for you, you must be brutally honest about yourself about your point of departure. You must sit down and analyze yourself in detail to decide exactly where you are today in each area.

Start at the Beginning

For example, if you decide to lose weight, the very first step you would take is to weigh yourself. From then on, you continually use that weight as your measure for whether or not you are making progress toward your goal.

If you decide to begin a personal exercise program, the first step you take is to determine how much you are exercising today. How many minutes per day and per week are you exercising and how intensely each time? What kind of exercises are you doing? Whatever your answer, it is important that you be as accurate as you possibly can. You then use this answer as a starting point and make your exercise plans for the future based on it.

Determine Your Hourly Rate

If you want to earn more money, the first step you take is to sit down and determine exactly how much you are earning right now. How much did you earn last year and the year before? How much will you earn this year? How much are you earning each month? The best measure of all is how much you are earning each hour right now.

You can determine your hourly rate by dividing your annual income by 2000, the approximate number of hours that you work each year. Even better, you can divide your monthly income by 172, the number of hours you work, on average, each month.

Many of my coaching clients calculate their hourly rate each week and compare it against previous weeks. They then set a goal to increase the value of what they do each hour so as to increase the amount they earn from then on. You should do the same.

Tight Time or Financial Measures Improve Performance

The tighter and more accurate your calculations regarding your income, or any other area, the better and faster you can improve in each one of them. For example, most people think in terms of monthly and annual salary. This is hard to analyze and increase. Conversely, the high performer thinks in terms of hourly rate, which is amenable to improvements on a minute-to-minute basis.

Since you are the president of your own personal services corporation, you should view yourself as being on your own payroll. Imagine you are paying yourself by the hour. Be just as demanding of yourself as you would be of someone else who was working for you. Refuse to do anything that doesn't pay your desired hourly rate.

Your Current Net Worth

If you have set a long-term financial goal, the next step is for you to determine exactly how much you are worth today in financial terms. If your goal is to become a millionaire in the years ahead, you must calculate exactly how much you have accumulated as of today's date.

Most people are confused or dishonest about this calculation. Your true dollar net worth is the amount that you would have left over if you sold everything you own today at what the market would pay and then paid off all your bills.

Many people place a high value on their personal possessions. They think that their clothes, cars, furniture, and electronics are worth a lot of money. But the true value of these items is usually not more than 10 percent or 20 percent of what they paid.

Develop Long-Term Financial Plans

For accurate financial planning, calculate your net worth today and then subtract that amount from your long-term financial goal. Divide the result by the number of years you intend to spend to achieve that financial goal. In this way, you will know exactly how much you have to save, invest, and accumulate each year in order to become financially independent.

Is your goal realistic, based on where you are today and the time that you have allocated to get where you want to go? If your goal is not realistic, force yourself to be completely honest and revise both your calculations and your projections.

Practice Zero-Based Thinking

When you begin to plan your long-term future, one of the most valuable exercises you can engage in is called "zero-based thinking." In zero-based thinking, you ask this question:

Knowing what I now know, is there anything that I am doing today that I wouldn't start again if I had to do it over?

No matter who you are or what you are doing, there are activities and relationships in your life that, knowing what you now know, you wouldn't get involved in.

It is difficult, if not impossible, for you to make progress in your life if you allow yourself to be held back by decisions you made in the past. If there is something in your life that you wouldn't get into again today, your next question is, How can I stop and how fast?

Evaluate Each Area of Your Life

Apply zero-based thinking to the people in both your business and personal life. Is there any *relationship* that, knowing what you now know, you wouldn't get into again? Is there any person you are working with or for who you wouldn't get involved with again? Be perfectly honest with yourself when you answer these questions.

Examine every aspect of your work life and career. Is there any job that you have taken that, knowing what you now know, you wouldn't take again? Is there any aspect of your business or work that you wouldn't embark upon again? Is there any activity, process, product, service, or expenditure in your business that, knowing what you now know, you wouldn't embark upon again today, if you had to do it over?

After people and work considerations, look at your investments. Is there any investment of time, money, or emotion that, knowing what you now know, you wouldn't make again today? If the answer is yes, how do you get out of it, and how fast?

Be Prepared to Make Necessary Changes

I have a good friend who was a golfer in high school and at his university. As a bachelor, he played golf several times a week. He organized his entire life around golf, even flying south in the winter to golf courses that had no snow on them.

Over time, he started and built a business, got married, and had children. But he was still "locked into" the idea of playing golf several times a week. Eventually, the enormous time commitment of playing golf began to affect his business, his married life, and his relationship with his children.

When the stress became too great, he sat down and zero-based his activities. He realized that, knowing what he now knew, in his current situation, the golf would have to be cut back dramatically if he was going to achieve other goals in his life that were now more important. By reducing his golfing time, he got his whole life back into balance in just a few weeks. How might this principle apply to you? What major time-consuming activities should you reduce or eliminate?

Circumstances Are Continually Changing

Fully 70 percent of the decisions that you make will turn out to be wrong in the fullness of time. When you made the decision or commitment, it was probably a good idea, based on the circumstances of the moment. But now, the situation may have changed and it is time to "zero-base" it again.

You can usually tell if you are in a zero-based thinking situation because of the stress that it causes. Whenever you are involved in something that knowing what you now know you wouldn't get into, you experience ongoing stress, aggravation, irritation, and anger.

Sometimes people spend an enormous amount of time trying to make a business or personal relationship succeed. But if you zero-base this relationship, the correct solution is often to get out of the relationship altogether. The only real question is whether or not you have the courage to admit that you were wrong and take the necessary steps to correct the situation.

What Is Holding You Back?

If you want to earn a certain amount of money, ask yourself, Why am I not earning this amount of money already? What is holding you back? What is the major reason that you are not already earning what you want to earn? Again, you must be perfectly honest with yourself.

Look around you and identify people who are earning the kind of money that you want to earn. What are they doing differently from you? What special skills and abilities have they developed that you have not yet developed? What skills and abilities do you need to acquire if you want to earn the same kind of money they are earning? If you are not sure, go and ask them. Find out. This is too important for guesswork or chance.

Determine Your Level of Skills and Ability

Do a skills inventory of yourself. First, identify the key result areas of your work. These are the tasks that you absolutely, positively have to fulfill in an excellent fashion in order to do your job well. What are they?

In every job there are seldom more than five to seven key result areas. These are critical tasks. You must be excellent at each one of them in order to do the whole job for which you are paid. You must be good at every one of these tasks if you want to earn the kind of money that you are capable of earning.

Here is an important discovery: Your *weakest* key skill sets the height at which you can use all your other skills and determines your income in your field. You can be absolutely excellent at everything except for one key skill, and that skill will hold you back every step of the way.

In what area, at which skill, are you the very best at what you do? What particular skill, or combination of skills, is responsible for your success in your career to date? What is it that you do as well or better than anyone else?

Identify Your Weakest Areas

Once you have answered these questions, look at yourself in the mirror and ask, "What are my weakest skill areas?" What is it that you do poorly that interferes with your ability to use your other skills? What do other people do better than you? Especially, what key skills do you lack that are essential for your success? Whatever they are, you need to identify them accurately and honestly and then make a plan to improve in each area. (We will discuss this in depth in a later chapter.)

Imagine Starting Over

When you embark on the achievement of any great goal, you should imagine that at any time you could start your career over again. Never allow yourself to feel locked in or trapped by a particular decision from the past. Keep focused on the future.

Many people today are walking away from their educations, their businesses, their industries, and their years of experience and starting something completely new and different. They are honest enough to recognize that there is a limited future in the direction they are going, and they are determined to try something where the future possibilities are far greater. You must do the same.

In doing a baseline assessment of yourself and your life, you must face the facts, whatever they are. As Harold Geneen of ITT once said, "Facts don't lie." Seek out the real facts, not the obvious facts, the apparent facts, the hoped-for facts, or the wished-for facts. The true facts are what you need to make good decisions.

Be Prepared to Reinvent Yourself

Take a hard look at your current company and industry and your current job situation. Take a hard look at your market relative to your competitors. In reinventing yourself, stand back and think about starting your career over again today, knowing what you now know.

Imagine that your job and your industry disappeared overnight. Imagine that you had to make brand new career choices. If you were starting over again today, with your special combination of talents and skills, what would you choose to do that is different from what you are doing now?

Your Most Valuable Asset

Your most valuable financial asset is your earning ability, your ability to apply your talents and skills in the marketplace. In reality, you could lose your home, your car, your bank account, and your furniture and be left with nothing but the clothes on your back. But as long as your earning ability was intact, you could walk across the street and begin generating a good living almost immediately.

Your earning ability is extremely precious to you. And your earning ability can be either an *appreciating* asset or a *depreciating* asset. Your earning ability can grow in value if you continue to invest in and develop it. It can decline in value if you begin to take it for granted and start to coast on the basis of what you have done in the past.

Bundle of Resources

See yourself as a "bundle of resources" capable of doing many different things. You have a wide variety of skills, abilities, knowledge, talents, education, and experience. There are many jobs and tasks that you could do, or learn to do, extremely well. Never allow yourself to get locked into a particular course of action, especially if you are not happy with the way your career is going today.

In mentally starting over, as though you were beginning your career anew, look deeply into yourself as well. What *good* habits do you have that are helping you and moving you toward your goals? What *bad* habits have you developed that may be holding you back? What are your very best qualities of character and personality? What are your weakest qualities? What new habits and qualities do you need to develop to get the very most out of yourself and what is your plan to begin developing them? What bad habits do you need to get rid of and replace with good habits?

Go from Good to Great

Jim Collins in his best-selling business book, *Good to Great,* says that you must be willing to ask the "brutal questions" of yourself and your business if you are going to identify and remove the obstacles that are preventing you from moving ahead. What are some of the brutal questions that you have to ask yourself before you launch wholeheartedly toward your goals?

Whenever I do strategic planning for a company, we start the session with four questions. First, Where are we *now?* We gather data and information from every part of the company to develop a crystal-clear picture of our starting point, especially with regard to sales, market position, and profitability.

Second, we ask, Where would we ideally like to be in the *future?* We idealize and practice future orientation. We imagine that we can make the company into anything we like in the years ahead, and we create a perfect vision of what the company would look like if we were successful in every respect.

Third, we ask, *How* did we get to where we are today? What did we do right? What would we do differently? What have been our biggest successes so far, and why did they occur? What have we failed at, and what were the reasons for it? As George Santayana wrote, "Those who cannot remember the past are doomed to repeat it."

The fourth question we ask and answer is always, What do we do now, to get from where we are to where we want to go? Based on our experience, what should we be doing more of or less of? What should we start doing that we are not doing today? What should we stop doing altogether?

Put Together Your Own Strategic Plan

The good news is that if we have answered the first three questions accurately, the strategic plan or blueprint comes together more easily than if we were trying to plan without being clear about where we were or how we got there.

There is an old saying, "Well begun is half done." Doctors say, "Accurate diagnosis is half the cure." Taking the time to honestly evaluate each part of your situation before you launch toward your goal will save you months and even years on your journey. In many cases, it will force you to reevaluate your goals in the light of superior analysis and knowledge. It will dramatically improve the speed at which you achieve your goals once you get going.

❖ START AT THE BEGINNING

1 Determine the reality of your current situation relative to your major goals. Where are you now and how far do you have to go?

2 Apply the zero-based thinking principle to every area of your life. What are you doing today that you wouldn't get involved with again if you had it to do over, knowing what you now know?

3 Do a complete financial analysis of your life. How much are you earning today, and how much are you worth? What are your goals in these areas?

4 Do a complete skills analysis of yourself and your work. Where are you good? Where do you need to improve?

5 Determine exactly how much you earn each hour and what it is you do to earn that amount. What do you have to do to increase your hourly rate in the months ahead?

6 Imagine your future was perfect in every way. What would have to happen to make that vision a reality?

9

Measure Your Progress

There is no road too long to the man who advances
deliberately and without undue haste; there are no
honors too distant to the man who prepares himself
for them with patience.

—JEAN DE LA BRUYÈRE

You have incredible mental powers that you habitually
fail to use to their full extent. By systematically setting goals
for your life and making detailed plans to achieve them, you
will save yourself years of hard work in reaching the same
level of success. Goal setting enables you to use vastly more
of your thinking powers than most other people.

Your conscious mind is the "head office" of your life. Its
role is to deal with the information in your environment,
identify it, analyze it, compare it against other information;
and then decide what actions to take.

But it is your subconscious mind that contains the great
powers that can enable you to accomplish vastly more than
you ever have before. At least 90 percent or more of your
mental powers are "below the surface." It is essential that
you learn to tap into these powers to motivate, stimulate, and
drive you forward toward the achievement of your goals.

Program Yourself with Goals

Your subconscious mind functions best with clear goals, specific tasks, deliberate measures, and firm deadlines. The more

of these you program into your subconscious computer, the better it functions for you and the more you will accomplish in a shorter period of time.

As you set your goals and begin moving toward them, it is essential that you establish a series of benchmarks or measures that you can use to evaluate your progress, day by day and hour by hour. The more clear and specific the measures you set, the more accurate you will be in hitting your targets on schedule.

Your subconscious mind requires a "forcing system," composed of deadlines that you have imposed on yourself for task accomplishment and goal attainment. Without a forcing system, it becomes easy for you to procrastinate and delay and to put off important tasks until much later, if you do them at all.

Three Keys to Peak Performance

The three keys to peak performance in achieving your goals are *commitment, completion,* and *closure.*

When you make a firm commitment to achieve a particular goal, and you put aside all excuses, it is very much like stepping on the accelerator of your subconscious mind. You will be more creative, determined, and focused than ever before. Great men and women are those who make clear, unequivocal commitments and then refuse to budge from them, no matter what happens.

Completion is the second ingredient in peak performance. There is an enormous difference between doing 95 percent of a task and doing 100 percent of a task. In fact, it is very common for people to work very hard up to the 90 percent or 95 percent level and then slack off and delay the final completion of the task. This is a temptation that you must fight against. You must continually force yourself, discipline yourself, to resist this natural tendency and push through to completion.

Nature's Wonder Drug

Every time you complete a task of any kind, your brain releases a small quantity of endorphins. This natural morphine gives you a sense of well-being and elation. It makes you feel happy and peaceful. It stimulates your creativity and improves your personality. It is nature's "wonder drug."

The more important the task that you complete is, the greater is the quantity of endorphins that your brain releases— very much like a reward for success and achievement. Over time, you can develop a *positive addiction* to the feelings of well-being that you receive from this "endorphin rush."

Even when you complete a *small* task, you feel happier. When you complete a *large* task, you feel happier still. When you finish the various steps on the way to the completion of a large task, at every achievement you get an endorphin rush. You feel continuously happy and exhilarated when you are working steadily toward the completion of an important job.

Create the Winning Feeling

Everyone wants to feel like a winner. And feeling like a winner requires that you *win.* You get a feeling of the winner by completing a task 100 percent. When you do this repeatedly, eventually you develop the habit of completing the tasks that you begin. When this habit of task completion locks in, your life will begin to improve in ways that you cannot today imagine.

In psychology, the reverse is always true. The "incomplete action" is a major source of stress and anxiety. In fact, much of the unhappiness that people experience is because they have not been able to discipline themselves to follow through and complete an important task or responsibility.

The Pain of Procrastination

If you have ever had a major assignment that you have put off, you know what I am referring to. The longer you wait to get started on an assignment and the closer the deadline approaches, the greater the stress you experience. It can start to keep you up at night and affect your personality. But when you finally launch into the task and push it through to completion, you feel a great sense of relief and well-being.

It is almost as if nature rewards you for everything that you do that is positive and life enhancing. At the same time, nature penalizes you with stress and dissatisfaction when you fail to do the tasks that move you toward the goals and results that are important to you.

The Balanced Scorecard

One of the most popular movements in modern management is toward a "balanced scorecard." Using these scorecards, every person at every level of the business is encouraged to identify the key measures that indicate success and then give themselves scores every day and every week in each of those key areas.

Here is an important point. The very act of identifying a number or score and then paying close attention to it will cause you to improve your performance in that area. For example, if someone were to tell you, before a meeting, that you were going to be evaluated on how well you listened in that meeting, your listening skills would improve dramatically within a few moments. You would listen far more carefully and attentively throughout the meeting because you knew that this behavior was being observed.

In the same way, whenever you select a goal, measure, or activity that is important to you and begin observing or paying attention to it in your day-to-day life, your performance in that area improves.

One of the most helpful actions you take in your own career is to set benchmarks and create scorecards, measures, and deadlines for every key task that you must complete on the way to one of your goals. In this way, you activate your subconscious forcing system. This forcing system will then motivate you and drive you, at an unconscious level, to start earlier, work harder, stay later, and get the job done.

Close the Loop

The third C, after commitment and completion, is "closure." This is the difference between an "open loop" and a "closed loop." Bringing closure to an issue in your personal or business life is absolutely essential for you to feel happy and in control of your situation.

Lack of closure—unfinished business, an incomplete action of any kind—is a major source of stress, dissatisfaction, and even failure in business. It consumes enormous amounts of physical and emotional energy.

The Key Ability

Perhaps the most important ability in the world of work is "depend-ability." Nothing will get you paid more and promoted faster than to develop a reputation for getting your tasks done quickly, well, and on schedule.

Whatever your goals, make a list of all the tasks that you will have to accomplish in the achievement of those goals. Put a deadline on every one of those tasks. Then work every day and every hour to hit your deadlines. Measure your progress each day. Speed up or slow down where necessary. But remember, you can't hit a target that you can't see. The greater clarity that you have with regard to deadlines and measures, the more you will accomplish and the faster you will get it done.

A goal or a decision without a deadline is merely a discussion. It has no energy behind it. It is like a bullet with no powder in the cartridge. Unless you establish deadlines to which you are committed, you will end up "firing blanks" in life and work.

Sometimes people ask, "What if I set a deadline and I don't achieve the goal by the deadline?"

Simple. Set another deadline and then another, if necessary. Deadlines are "best-guess" estimates of when a task will be completed. The more you set and work toward deadlines, the more accurate you will become in predicting the time necessary to complete them. You will become better and better at achieving your goals and completing your tasks on schedule every time.

Eating an Elephant

You have heard the question, "How do you eat an elephant?"

The answer is, "One bite at a time."

This metaphor applies to achieving any big goal, as well. How do you achieve a huge goal? You accomplish it one step, one task, one measure at a time.

Break your long-term goals down into annual, monthly, weekly, and even hourly goals. Even if your long-term goal is financial independence, look for a way to break that down into how you are going to use each hour of the coming day in such a way that long-term financial independence is far more likely.

If you want to increase your income, you know that all income is a result of "added value." Look at everything you do and then ask yourself how you could add more value so that you can be worth more than you are earning today.

Identify Your Most Valuable Task

Ask your boss, "What one thing do I do that is more valuable than anything else?" Whatever his or her answer, look for ways to perform more and more of that task and to get better and better at doing it.

It is absolutely amazing how much you can accomplish if you break your tasks down into bite-sized pieces, set deadlines, and then do one piece at a time, every single day. You have heard the old saying, "By the yard it's hard; but inch by inch, anything's a cinch."

Continuous and Never Ending Improvement

If you want to increase your hourly rate and your income, look for ways to get a little bit better at the most important tasks you do, every single day. Read one hour per day in your field. Listen to audio programs on your way to and from work. Take additional courses whenever you can. These activities will propel your entire career onto the fast-track. When you invest an extra one or two hours per day in self-improvement, the cumulative effect on your greater ability to get results can be extraordinary.

Get Healthy and Fit

If you want to lose weight, there is a simple five-word formula: eat less and exercise more.

If you discipline yourself to eat a little bit less but eat higher quality foods, and simultaneously exercise a little bit more each day, you can get into the rhythm of losing one ounce per day. No matter how much you weigh today, if you lose one ounce each day, that will equal about two pounds per month. Two pounds per month will be twenty-four pounds per year. In no time at all, you can retrain your body and your appetite so that you lose the weight and keep it off for the rest of your life.

Save Your Pennies and the Dollars Will Save Themselves

If you want to become wealthy, begin to question every single expense. Set a goal to save $3, $5, or $10 per day. Put this money away in a savings account and never touch it. As it grows, invest it carefully in well-chosen mutual funds or index funds. Make daily, weekly, and monthly saving and investment into a habit, and keep it up for the rest of your working life.

In no time at all, you will become comfortable living on slightly less than you are spending today. As your income increases, increase the amount that you save. In a few weeks, a few months, a few years, you will be out of debt and have a large amount of money put away and working for you. A few years down the road, you will be financially independent.

Become a Learned Person

If you read fifteen minutes each evening, rather than watching television, you will complete about fifteen books per year. If you read the great classics of English literature for fifteen minutes each day, in seven years you will have read the one hundred greatest books ever written. You will be one of the best-educated and most erudite people of your generation. And you can achieve this just by reading fifteen minutes each evening before you go to bed.

Increase Your Income

If you are in sales and you want to increase your income, keep careful track of how many calls, how many presentations, how many proposals, and how many sales you are making each day, each week, and each month. Then set a goal to increase your number of calls, presentations, and proposals per day. Set a goal to increase your number of sales each week and each month. Every day, measure yourself against your own standards.

If You Measure It, You Can Manage It

In each area of your life, analyze your activities carefully and select a specific number that, more than anything else, determines your level of success in that area. Then focus all of your attention, all day long, on that specific number. The very act of focused attention will cause you to perform better in that area, both consciously and unconsciously.

If you want to be healthier, you could focus on the number of minutes per week that you exercise or the number of calories per day that you eat. If you want to be successful financially, you could focus on the amount you earn each hour or the amount that you save each month. If you want to be successful in sales, you could focus on the number of calls you make each day or the number of sales or the size of the sales you make each month. If you want to be successful in your relationships, you could focus on the number of minutes that you spend face to face with the most important people in your life, each day and each week.

You have heard the saying, "What gets measured gets done." There is another saying: "If you can't measure it, you can't manage it." Your ability to set specific measures on your goals, keep an accurate record and track your performance each day, will assure that you achieve your goals exactly when you have decided to—or even before.

▨ | MEASURE YOUR PROGRESS

1 Determine a single measure that you can use to grade your progress and success in each area of your life. Refer to it daily.

2 Determine the most important part of your job as it affects your income, and measure your daily activities in that area.

3 Set a minimum, specific amount for daily, weekly, monthly saving and investment, and discipline yourself to put away those amounts.

4 Break every large goal down into measurable, controllable parts and then focus on accomplishing each part on a fixed deadline.

5 Make it a game with yourself to set benchmarks, measures, scorecards, targets, and deadlines for every goal, and then focus on those numbers and dates. The goals will take care of themselves.

6 Resolve to accomplish at least one specific part of a larger goal each day, and never miss a day.

10

Remove the Roadblocks

The person interested in success has to learn to view failure as a healthy, inevitable part of the process of getting to the top.

—JOYCE BROTHERS

How many times do you think that people try to achieve their new goals before they give up? The average is less than one time. Most people give up before they even make the first try. And the reason they give up is because of all the obstacles, difficulties, problems, and roadblocks that immediately appear as soon as they decide to do something that they have never done before.

The fact is that successful people fail far more often than unsuccessful people. Successful people try more things, fall down, pick themselves up, and try again—over and over again—before they finally win. Unsuccessful people try a few things, if they try at all, and very soon quit and go back to what they were doing before.

Temporary Failure Always Precedes Success

You should expect to fail and fall short many times before you achieve your goals. You should look upon failure and temporary defeat as a part of the price that you pay on your road to the success that you will inevitably achieve. As Henry

Ford once said, "Failure is merely an opportunity to more intelligently begin again."

Once you have decided upon your goal, ask yourself, Why am I not there already? What is holding you back? Why haven't you achieved that goal up to now?

Identify all the obstacles that stand between you and your goal. Write down every single detail that you can think of that might be blocking you or slowing you down from moving ahead.

Think in Terms of Solutions

Remember, "You become what you think about most of the time." In the area of problems and difficulties, successful people have a particular way of thinking that we call "solution orientation."

Successful people think about *solutions* most of the time. Unsuccessful people think about problems and difficulties most of the time. Solution-oriented people are constantly looking for ways to get over, around, and past the obstacles that stand in their way. Problem-oriented people talk continuously about their problems, who or what caused them, how unhappy or angry they are, and how unfortunate it is that they have occurred. Solution-oriented people, on the other hand, simply ask the question, How can we solve this? and then take action to deal with the problem.

Between you and anything you want to accomplish you will always find problems or obstacles of some kind. This is why success is sometimes defined as *the ability to solve problems.* Personal leadership is the ability to solve problems. So is effectiveness. All men and women who accomplish anything of importance are people who have developed the ability to solve the problems that stand between them and their goals.

Problem Solving Is a Skill

Fortunately, problem solving is a skill, like riding a bicycle or typing with a typewriter or keyboard, which you can learn. The more you focus on solutions, the more and better solutions will come to you. The better you get at solving problems, the faster you will be at solving each subsequent problem. As you get better and faster at solving problems, you will attract even bigger and more expensive problems to solve. Eventually, you will be solving problems that can have significant financial consequences for you and others. This is the way the world works.

The fact is that you have the ability to solve any problem or to overcome any obstacle on the path to your goal if you desire the goal intensely enough. You have within you, right now, all the intelligence and ability you will ever need to overcome any obstacle that could possibly hold you back.

The Theory of Constraints

One of the most important breakthroughs in thinking in the last few decades was described by Eliyahu Goldratt in his book *The Goal* as "the theory of constraints." This theory says that between you and anything you want to accomplish there is a constraint, or limiting factor, that determines how fast you get to where you want to go.

For example, if you are driving down a freeway and traffic construction is narrowing all the cars into a single lane, this bottleneck or choke point becomes the constraint that determines how fast you will get to your destination. The speed at which you pass through this bottleneck will largely determine the speed of your entire journey.

In accomplishing any major goal, there is always a constraint or bottleneck you must get through as well. Your job is to identify it accurately and then focus all of your energies on alleviating that key constraint. Your ability to remove this bottleneck or deal with this limiting factor can help you move ahead faster than perhaps any other step you can take.

Internal versus External Constraints

The 80/20 rule applies to the constraints between you and your goals. This rule says that 80 percent of your constraints will be *within* yourself. Only 20 percent of your constraints will be outside of yourself, contained in other people and situations. To put it another way, it is you *personally* who is usually the major roadblock that is setting the speed at which you achieve any goal that you set for yourself.

For most people, this is hard to accept. But successful people are more concerned with *what* is right rather than *who* is right. Successful people are more concerned with the truth of the situation and what they can do to solve the problem, than they are with protecting their egos.

Look into Yourself

Ask yourself, What is it *in me* that is holding me back? Look deep within yourself and identify the key constraints in your personality, temperament, skills, abilities, habits, education, or experience that might be holding you back from achieving the goals that you have set for yourself. Ask the brutal questions. Be completely honest with yourself.

The primary obstacles between you and your goals are usually mental. They are psychological and emotional in character. They are within yourself rather than within the situation around you. And it is with these mental obstacles that you must begin if you want to achieve everything that is possible for you.

Two Major Obstacles to Success

The two major obstacles to success and achievement are *fear* and *doubt*. It is first of all the fear of failure, poverty, loss, embarrassment, or rejection that holds most people back from trying in the first place. This is why the average number of times that people try to achieve a new goal is less than one. As soon as they think of the goal, these fears overwhelm them and, like a bucket of water on a small fire, extinguish their desire completely.

The second mental obstacle, closely aligned to fear, is self-doubt. We doubt our own abilities. We compare ourselves unfavorably to others and think that others are somehow better, smarter, and more competent than we are. We think, "I'm not good enough." We feel inadequate and inferior to the challenges of achieving the great goals that we so much want to accomplish.

Negative Emotions Can Be Unlearned

Fortunately, if there is anything good about doubt and fear it is that they are both *learned* emotions. Have you ever seen a negative baby? Children come into the world with no doubts or fears at all. And whatever has been learned can be *unlearned* through practice and repetition.

The primary antidotes to doubt and fear are *courage* and *confidence*. The higher your level of courage and confidence, the lower will be your levels of fear and doubt and the less effect these negative emotions will have on your performance and behavior.

The Keys to Courage and Confidence

The way that you develop courage and confidence is with *knowledge* and *skill*. Most fear and doubt arises out of ignorance and feelings of inadequacy of some kind. The more you learn what you need to know to achieve your goals, the less fear you will feel on the one hand and the more courage and confidence you will feel on the other.

Think about learning to drive for the first time. You were probably extremely tense and nervous and made a lot of mistakes. You may have driven erratically and been a danger to yourself and others. But over time, as you mastered the knowledge and skills of driving, you became better and better and your confidence increased.

Today, you can quite comfortably get into your car and drive across the country with no fear or worry at all. You are so competent at driving that you can do it well without even thinking about it. The same principles apply to any skills you need to learn to achieve any goal you can set for yourself.

Powerful versus Powerless

Dr. Martin Seligman of the University of Pennsylvania spent more than 25 years studying the phenomenon of what he called "learned helplessness." What Seligman concluded, after interviewing and studying many thousands of people, was that more than 80 percent of the population suffers from learned helplessness to some degree and occasionally to a very high degree.

People suffering from learned helplessness feel that they are incapable of achieving their goals or improving their lives. The most common manifestation of learned helplessness is contained in the words "I can't." Whenever the victims of learned helplessness are offered an opportunity, possibility, or new goal, they immediately respond by saying, "I can't." They then go on to give all the reasons why a particular goal or objective is not possible for them.

"I can't move ahead in my career. I can't get a better job. I can't take time off to study. I can't save money. I can't lose weight. I can't start my own business. I can't start a second-income business. I can't change or improve my relationship. I can't get my time under control."

Whatever it is, they always have a self-limiting reason that immediately slams on the brakes of their potential. It short-circuits any attempt or desire to set a new goal or to change things in any way. Another famous observation of Henry Ford was, "If you believe you can do a thing or you believe you cannot, in either case, you are probably right."

Unlearning Helplessness

Learned helplessness is usually caused by destructive criticism in childhood, negative experiences growing up, and failures experienced as an adult. The way you get over this natural tendency to sell yourself short is by setting small goals, making plans, and working on them each day. In this way, you gradually develop greater courage and confidence, like building up a muscle. As you become more confident in yourself and your abilities, you can set even larger goals. Over time, your doubts and fears will weaken and your courage and confidence will grow and become the dominant force in your thinking. Eventually, with a record of successes behind you, it won't be long before you become *unstoppable*.

The Trap of the Comfort Zone

The second mental obstacle that you need to overcome is the "comfort zone." Many people become complacent with their current situations. They become so comfortable in a particular job or relationship or at a particular salary or level of responsibility that they become reluctant to make any changes at all, even for the better.

The comfort zone is a major obstacle to ambition, desire, determination, and accomplishment. People who get stuck in a comfort zone, if it's combined with learned helplessness, are almost impossible to help in any way. Don't let this happen to you.

Set Big, Challenging Goals

The way that you get out of your comfort zone and break loose from learned helplessness is by setting big, challenging goals. You then break these goals down into specific tasks, set deadlines, and work on them every day. Like an ice floe breaking up in the spring, soon the sluggishness and lethargy of learned helplessness and the comfort zone break up and you begin moving faster and faster toward accomplishing more and more of what is possible for you.

Organize Your Obstacles by Priority

Once you have made a list of all the obstacles that are standing in the way of your achieving your major goals, organize the obstacles by priority. What is the largest single obstacle?

If you could wave a magic wand and remove one major obstacle from your path, which one obstacle, if removed, would help you the most in moving ahead more rapidly?

Management consultant Ian Mitroff has an interesting set of observations with regard to problem solving and the removal of obstacles. He says, "Whatever the problem, define it several different ways before you attempt to solve it. Beware of any problem for which there is only one definition, or only one solution."

When you ask the question, with regard to your goal, Why am I not there already? what answer comes to mind? What is holding you back? What is standing in your way? It is at this point that you have to *drill down* to determine the correct obstacle before you begin taking steps to remove it.

You do this by asking the question, *What else* could be the problem? after each definition of the problem.

Conducting a Sales Analysis

In my work with corporations, and with individuals, we start off with the goal of doubling profits or income. I then suggest that they ask themselves, Why is it that our profits or our income are not twice as high already? By repeated questioning, we often come up with an answer that is quite different from the obvious answer.

Here is an example of the questioning process:

"We are not making enough sales." *What else* could be the problem?

"Our individual sales are not large enough per customer." *What else* could be the problem?

"Our advertising is not attracting enough customers." *What else* could be the problem?

As you can see, whichever of these obstacles turns out to be the correct problem will require a completely different course of action to solve it. If we don't have enough sales, our solution is to increase the number of sales. If our sales are not large enough per customer, our solution is to increase the size of sale per customer. If our advertising is not drawing enough customers, our solution is to improve the quality of our advertising in some way.

Keep Drilling Deeper

You could say, "Our customers are not buying enough from us." *What else* could be the problem?

"Our customers are not buying frequently enough from us." *What else* could be the problem?

"Our salespeople are not selling enough to our customers." This could lead to totally revamping the quality of the sales force through better recruiting, training, and management. *What else* could be the problem?

"Our customers are buying too many of our products from our competitors." *What else* could be the problem?

"Our competitors are selling too many of their products to our customers." This answer forces you to ask, "What value or benefit do our prospective customers see in purchasing from our competitors? How could we offset this perceived benefit?" *What else* could be the problem?

"We are not making enough profit on our sales." *What else* could be the problem?

"It costs us too much to make each sale." What else could be the problem? And so on. Each new definition of the problem suggests different ways that the goal of increased sales or profitability could be achieved.

Apply the Right Solution to the Right Problem

In the business book *The McKinsey Way,* describing the management consulting practices of McKinsey and Company, the authors point out that one of the greatest wastes of time and money is in applying the wrong solution to the wrong problem in the first place. This can apply to your problems and obstacles as well.

When you identify the constraints you face or the reasons that you are not achieving your personal income goals, each definition will lead to a different set of solutions. They each require that you think in different ways.

In your personal life, it is the same. The accuracy with which you identify the obstacles or bottlenecks that are holding you back will determine the appropriateness of the various steps that you can take to remove or alleviate those obstacles.

Increasing Your Income

You could start off by stating the problem in this way: "I'm not earning enough money." *What else* is the problem?

"I'm not contributing enough value to be worth more money." *What else* could be the problem?

"I'm not good enough at what I do to be capable of getting results that are worth more than I'm earning today." *What else* could be the problem?

"I don't use my time efficiently enough during the work day." *What else* could be the problem?

"I spend my evenings watching television, my weekends socializing, and I seldom read or learn anything that would help me to be better at my job."

Aha! Now you have found the *real* problem. Now you have a clear idea of what you have to do differently if you are going to solve your original problem, which was to earn more money.

Define the Obstacle as a Goal

Once you have determined the major obstacle that is holding you back, rewrite that obstacle as a positive goal. For example, you could now say, "My goal is to continually upgrade my skills and abilities so that I am in the top 10 percent of money earners in my field."

You then make a list of all the steps that you could take to upgrade your knowledge and skills, improve your time management, increase your efficiency and effectiveness, and make more sales for your company.

You set deadlines and measures next to each step. You then select one key task and take action on it immediately. From then on, you hold your own feet to the fire. You become your own taskmaster. You discipline and drive yourself to do what you must do to become the kind of person you must become in order to achieve the goals that you have set for yourself.

This exercise of identifying what is holding you back and then setting a clear, written goal to remove that obstacle puts you back in control of your own life.

By following through on your resolution, you virtually guarantee your ultimate success and the achievement of almost any goal you can set for yourself.

Strive for Accuracy

If you have any questions or concerns about the accuracy of your problem definition, discuss it with someone you know and trust. Put your ego aside. Invite honest feedback and criticism. Be open to the possibility that you have fundamental flaws and weaknesses that are standing in the way of your realizing your full potential. Be brutally honest with yourself.

Once your problem or obstacle is clear to you, ideas, opportunities, and answers will come to you from various sources. You will begin to attract the kinds of resources that will help you to overcome the obstacle or difficulty—either within yourself or within the situation around you—and move you more rapidly toward your goal.

Almost Every Problem Can Be Solved

Remember the old poem, "For every problem under the sun, there is a solution or there is none. If there is a solution, go and find it. If there isn't, never mind it."

For every problem or obstacle that is standing between you and what you want to accomplish, there is usually a solution of some kind somewhere. Your job is to be absolutely clear about what sets the speed at which you achieve your goal and then focus your time and attention on alleviating that constraint. By removing your major obstacle, you will often make more progress in a few months than most other people might make in several years.

REMOVE THE ROADBLOCKS

1 Identify a major goal and then ask, "Why aren't I there already? What is holding me back?" List everything you can think of.

2 Look into yourself and face the possibility that it is your own fears and doubts that are your biggest roadblocks to success.

3 Identify the constraint or limiting factor, in yourself or the situation, that sets the speed at which you achieve your goal.

4 Develop several definitions of your major problem or obstacle. Ask, "What else is the problem?"

5 Define your best solution as a goal, set a deadline, make a plan of action, and then get busy on your plan. Work on it every day until the problem is solved or the obstacle is removed.

11

Become an Expert in Your Field

The uncommon man is merely the common man thinking and dreaming of success and in more fruitful areas.

—MELVIN POWERS

Like the army recruiting poster, one of your goals is to "Be all you can be." The market only pays excellent rewards for excellent performance. It pays average rewards for average performance and below average rewards, under achievement, failure, and frustration for below average results.

In our economic system, your income will be determined by three factors: first, what you do; second, how well you do it; and third, the difficulty of replacing you.

One quality of the most successful people is that at a certain point in their careers they decided to "commit to excellence." They decided to be the best at what they do. They decided to pay any price, make any sacrifice, and invest any amount of time necessary to become very good in their chosen fields. And as a result of this decision, they pulled away from the pack of average performers and moved themselves upward into the income category where today they earn three, four, five, and ten times as much as their peers who have not made this commitment.

The 80/20 Rule Revisited

When I started my sales career many years ago, someone told me about the 80/20 rule as it applied to sales. He said that 20 percent of the salespeople made 80 percent of the money. This means that 80 percent of the salespeople make only 20 percent of the money, and they have to divide it amongst themselves. At that point, many years ago, I decided that I would prefer to be a member of the top 20 percent rather than the *bottom* 80 percent. This decision changed my life forever.

Because I had come from a difficult childhood and received below average grades in school, I grew up with a poor self-image and a low level of self-confidence. It never occurred to me that I could be good at anything. If ever I attempted something and did it well, I immediately dismissed it as an accident or a lucky break. For years, I saw myself as an average or below average performer in any job I worked at.

The Great Insight

Then one day I had a sudden flash of insight. I realized that everyone who is in the top 10 percent of their field started in the bottom 10 percent. Everyone who is doing well today was once doing poorly. Everyone who is at the front of the buffet line of life started at the back of the line. And even more importantly, it dawned on me that whatever others have done, within reason, I could do as well. And this turns out to be true for just about everyone.

No one is better than you and no one is smarter than you. People are just better or smarter in different areas. In addition, all business skills are *learnable*. People who are doing better in some area of business have learned the essential skills, in combination with other skills, before you have. If you are not achieving what others are achieving, it simply means that you have just not learned these skills yet!

The Iron Law of Self-Development

Here was another breakthrough realization for me: *You can learn anything you need to learn to achieve any goal you can set for yourself.* There are no real limits on what you can accomplish, except for the limits that you place on your own mind and imagination. If you decide to become excellent, to join the top 10 percent of people in your field, nothing on earth can stop you from getting there, except yourself.

Will it be easy? Of course not! I do not use the word "easy" in this book. Everything worthwhile takes a long time and a lot of work to accomplish. But it is possible if you want it badly enough and are willing to work long enough. And it is worth every bit of the effort once you get there!

Les Brown, the motivational speaker, says, "To achieve something that you have never achieved before, you must become someone that you have never been before."

Johann Wolfgang von Goethe, the German philosopher, said, "To have more, you must first be more."

Once you decide to become one of the best people in your field, the only question you ask is, How do I achieve it? The very fact that hundreds of thousands, and even millions, of people have gone from the bottom to the top in every field is ample proof that you can do it as well. Many of these people, if not most of them, may not even have the natural talents and abilities that you have. In most areas of life, it is more hard work and dedication than natural ability and talent that lead to excellence and great success.

Is Education Essential for Success?

In an analysis of the members of the Forbes 400, the 400 richest men and women in America, conducted a couple of years ago, researchers found that a person who dropped out of high school and who made it into the Forbes 400 was worth, on average, $333 million more than those who had completed college or university.

The reason I mention this is because many people feel that if they didn't get good grades in school they are permanently limited in what they can accomplish later in life. Nothing could be further from the truth. Some of the wealthiest, most successful men and women in America, and throughout the world, did poorly in school.

Remember the question, "How do you eat an elephant?" and the answer, "One bite at a time." This is the same way that you become absolutely excellent at what you do. You move to the top one step, one skill, one small improvement at a time.

Appreciating or Depreciating Asset?

The fact is that your current level of knowledge and skill is becoming obsolete at a faster rate today than ever before. I mentioned earlier that your "earning ability" can be an appreciating or a depreciating asset, depending upon whether or not you are upgrading it or simply allowing it to become obsolete. This is a choice you are making, or failing to make, every day.

The good news is that when you start to aggressively upgrade your knowledge and skills on the road to becoming one of the best people in your field, it will be as if you are in a race and you are the only one who is really running. You very soon move ahead of the pack and into the lead position. Meanwhile, most of your competitors are simply strolling along, doing just what they need to do to keep their jobs. The idea of committing to excellence has never even occurred to them.

Identify the Knowledge You Will Need

You begin your journey to excellence by asking the question, What additional knowledge, skills, and information will I need to lead my field in the months and years ahead?

Project yourself forward three to five years and imagine that you are one of the very best, highest paid people in your industry. What would have to have happened? What would you have to have done, learned, or accomplished to reach this point? What skills would you have had to master to lead your field?

Make a Career Move

Once upon a time, I had a good friend who was a lawyer in a small firm. His father had been a lawyer so he had taken law when he went to the university. When he got out of school in his early 20s, he began practicing law amongst his friends and associates. But he soon decided that law was not for him. He decided to make a career in business instead.

By this time he was about twenty-six years old. In the face of considerable opposition, he gathered all his resources and concentrated single-mindedly on getting into Harvard University to attend its MBA program. It took him two years, but he finally achieved it. It then took him two more years to complete the required courses and graduate with a coveted Harvard MBA.

He returned to his home city and interviewed for various jobs, finally taking an entry-level management position at a rapidly growing airline. It turned out to be a perfect career move. Within ten years he was the president of the airline and earning ten times as much as any of the lawyers that he had graduated with some years before. He became one of the youngest and most respected executives in charge of a major company in the country.

You Will Have Multiple Jobs and Careers

It is estimated that on average a person starting work today will have fourteen full-time jobs lasting two years or more and four or five full-time careers in completely different businesses or industries. Fully forty million Americans will be *contingency* workers for most of their careers. They will never work long-term for a single company but will instead move from company to company doing professional or technical jobs.

It is almost inevitable that your career will change continually as you grow and mature. You must be constantly looking down the road and thinking about the skills and competencies you will need to earn the kind of money you want to earn in the years ahead.

Identify Your Key Result Areas

As I mentioned before, every job is made up of about five to seven key result areas. In sales, for example, these seven key result areas consist of first, prospecting; second, establishing rapport; third, identifying needs; fourth, presenting solutions; fifth, answering objections; sixth, closing the sale; and seventh, getting resales and referrals from satisfied customers.

If you are in sales, you should give yourself a grade of one to ten, with one being the lowest and ten being the highest, in each of these areas. You need to have a minimum score of seven across the board to be in the top 20 percent of your field.

Once you have graded yourself in these seven areas, you should take the list to your boss or, even better, to one of your customers and ask that person to give you a grade as well. This could be a real eye-opener for you. Very often, the way you evaluate yourself is much different and higher than the way you are evaluated by others.

Whatever your final grades, you must then select your weakest key skill and work on that skill so that it is equal or greater than the others. Your weakest key skill sets the height of your income and determines how fast and how far you go in your career.

Move onto the Fast Track

Here is a great question for the rest of your working life: **What one skill, if you developed and did it in an excellent fashion, would have the greatest positive impact on your career?** This should become your focal point for personal and professional development.

If you are at all unsure about the answer to this question, go to your boss and ask him or her. Ask your coworkers. Ask your staff. Ask your spouse and your friends. It is absolutely essential that you find out the answer to this question and then focus all of your energies on improving your performance in this particular area.

This becomes your major definite purpose for personal and professional improvement. Write it down, set a deadline, make a plan, take action on your plan, and then do something every day to get better in this particular skill.

Once you have achieved mastery in your weakest key result area, then ask the question again: Now, what one skill will help me the most? And whatever your answer to that question, go to work on that skill until you achieve mastery in that area as well.

The highest paid people in every field score an eight, nine, or ten across the board in each of their key result areas. This must also be your goal.

The Excellent Executive

If you are in management, seven key result areas determine your success or failure at your job. These are (1) planning, (2) organizing, (3) staffing, (4) delegating, (5) supervising, (6) measuring, and (7) reporting.

All successful managers are excellent in every one of these areas. All unsuccessful managers are weak in one or more of these areas. A serious weakness in any one of these key result areas can be fatal to your success in your work.

For example, if you were absolutely excellent in every part of managing except for delegating, that would hold you back every day of your career. I have worked with managers who were so poor at delegating that they could get nothing done. They eventually had to be fired because of the damage they were causing to the rest of the business.

Give yourself a grade of one to ten in each of these key result areas. Ask people around you to grade you as well. And be honest. Seek the truth rather than a diplomatic answer from a polite coworker.

Perform a 360-Degree Analysis

One of the popular management tools being used today is called "360-degree analysis." In this type of analysis, a survey is given to several people who report to a particular manager. The survey is filled out anonymously and all the surveys are returned to an outside consultant who summarizes the answers. This summary is then given to the manager so that he or she can see how he or she is perceived by others. It often comes as quite a shock to the manager.

For example, the manager will say, "I make careful and thoughtful decisions." But the staff will say, "He is weak, indecisive, and insecure when it comes to making decisions."

In a recent management study, 75 percent of all managers rated themselves in the top 25 percent in terms of effectiveness. Most managers rated themselves in the top 20 percent in terms of personality and intelligence, as well. We have a natural tendency to rate ourselves very highly, no matter what the quality or characteristic. This is why it is so helpful for a person to be rated by his or her peers on a regular basis.

Set Personal Improvement as a Goal

Once you have determined the key result area where you want and need to improve the most, set it as a goal, make a plan, determine a standard, and set a deadline. Then, go to work to improve yourself in that area every day. In a week, a month, or a year, you will be absolutely excellent in that skill area. You will have become an expert.

Accept Yourself the Way You Are

One of the most popular business books in recent years is called *Now, Discover Your Strengths!* This book follows from an earlier best-seller, *First, Break All the Rules!* The common conclusion of both of these books is that "People don't change."

You are born with certain natural skills, abilities, tendencies, strengths, weaknesses, and talents. These emerge in early life and usually crystallize in your late teens. They do not change very much over the course of your lifetime.

One of the most important steps you take in your career is to identify what it is that you are really good at, or what you can become good at, and then put your whole heart into becoming excellent in that area.

Mary Parker Follett, a management consultant in the 1920s, once wrote, "The very best direction to ride a horse is in the direction it is going." The very best way to develop yourself is in the direction of your natural talents and interests. Jim Cathcart, the author and speaker, says, "Nurture your nature." This is extremely important advice that you should follow throughout your career.

You are put on this earth with special talents and abilities that make you unique and different from all other people who have ever lived. Throughout your life, you have often found yourself drawn to an area of activity where your special talents and abilities have enabled you to accomplish more and to enjoy what you are doing at a higher level than anything else you could do. One of your great goals in life is to identify and isolate the one or two skills that you can do better, and enjoy more, than anything else, and then concentrate on becoming absolutely excellent in those areas.

Develop Your Talents

Michael Jordan, the basketball player, once said, "Everybody has talent, but ability takes hard work." The poet Longfellow once wrote, "The great tragedy of the average man is that he goes to his grave with his music still in him."

You could struggle for years at a job for which you were ill-suited and then find yourself in the perfect field and make more progress in a couple of years than you had made in the twenty years preceding.

Napoleon Hill once wrote that the key to success in America is for you to "find out what you really love to do, and then find a way to make a good living doing it."

Most self-made millionaires say, "I never worked a day in my life." What they did was to find out what they really enjoyed, and then they did more and more of it.

Identify Your Special Talents

There are eight ways for you to identify and determine your special talents and what you are uniquely suited to do. Here they are:

First, you will always be the best and happiest at something that you *love to do*. If you could afford it, you would do it without pay. It brings out the very best in you and you get a tremendous amount of satisfaction and enjoyment when you are engaged in that particular work.

Second, *you do it well*. You seem to have a natural ability to perform in this area.

Third, this talent has been responsible for *most of your success and happiness in life,* up until now. From an early age, it has been something that you have enjoyed doing and brought you the greatest rewards and compliments from other people.

Fourth, it is something that was *easy for you to learn and easy to do*. In fact, it was so easy to learn that you actually forget when and how you learned it. You just found yourself doing it easily and well one day.

Fifth, it *holds your attention.* It absorbs you and fasci-
nates you. You like to think about it, read about it, talk
about it, and find out more about it. It seems to attract you
like a moth to a flame.

Sixth, you *love to learn about it* and become better at it
all your life. You have a deep inner desire to really excel in
this particular area.

Seventh, when you do it, *time stands still.* You can often
work in your area of special talent for long periods without
eating or sleeping, hour after hour, because you get so involved in it.

And eighth, you really *admire and respect other people*
who are good at what you are most suited to do. You want
to be like them and be around them and emulate them in
every way.

If the above descriptions apply to anything that you are
doing now, or anything that you have done in the past, they
can lead you into what you were uniquely put on this earth
to do, to your "heart's desire."

You Are Born to Excel

Your natural talents are inborn and easy to develop. They are
programmed into your subconscious mind. They are what
you were put on this earth to do. Your job is to discover this
area of natural talent and ability and then develop it
throughout your life.

Many skills are complementary. They are dependent on
each other. This means that you must have one skill at a certain level in order to use your other skills at a higher level.
Sometimes you have to learn and develop skills that you do
not particularly love and enjoy. But this is the price you pay
to be able to achieve excellence in your chosen field.

One Skill Away

Here is the rule: You could be only one skill away from doubling your productivity, performance, and income. You may only need to bring up your skill level in one area for you to be able to use all of your other skills at a higher level.

Remember that all business skills are learnable. Business skills are not genetically determined. If you need to learn any business skill to realize and utilize your full potential, you can learn it by practice and repetition.

Avoid the Trap of the Poor Performer

It is quite common that if you are weak in a particular skill, you will avoid taking action in that skill. You will fall into the trap of "learned helplessness." You will say, "I'm not really very good in that area." Or, "I don't have any natural talent or ability in that skill."

But this is merely rationalization and justification. If the skill is important enough to you, you can learn it. The very worst decision of all is for you to allow yourself to be held back for months or years because you lack a single, simple skill that is readily learnable through dedication and determination. Don't let this happen to you.

Excellence Is a Journey

There is an old saying: "Anything worth doing well is worth doing poorly at first." It is not practice that makes perfect; it is *imperfect* practice that eventually makes perfect.

Whenever you start something new, you can expect to do it poorly. You will feel clumsy and awkward at first. You will feel inadequate and inferior. You will often feel silly and embarrassed. But this is the price that you pay to achieve excellence in your field. You will always have to pay the price of success, and that price often involves the hard work of mastering a difficult skill that you need to move to the top of your field.

Wave Your Magic Wand

Use the magic wand technique. Imagine that you could wave a magic wand and be absolutely excellent at any particular skill. What would it be? If you could wave a magic wand and have any wish at all with regard to your talents and skills, what would you wish for?

Your answer to these questions will often be an indication of the new goals that you have to set with regard to the skills and abilities that you need to develop to be the best at what you do.

Become a lifelong "do-it-to-yourself" project. Be prepared to invest one, two, or three years to become absolutely excellent in a critical area. Be willing to pay any price, make any sacrifice to be the best at what you do.

The Three-Plus-One Formula

The three-plus-one formula for mastering any skill is simple, and it works every single time. First, read in the skill area each day, even if only for fifteen to thirty minutes. Knowledge is cumulative. The more you read and learn, the more confident you will become that you can do this job in an excellent fashion.

Second, listen to educational audio programs on the subject in your car. Average drivers today spend five hundred to one thousand hours each year in their cars driving around during the day. Turn driving time into learning time. You can become one of the best educated people in your field by simply listening to audio programs in your car rather than music.

Third, attend seminars and workshops on your subject. Many people's lives have been changed completely by attendance at a single one- or two-day seminar on a key subject. Forever after, they were completely different in that area.

And the final factor is to practice what you learn at the earliest possible opportunity. Every time you hear a good idea, take action on it. The person who hears one idea and takes action on it is more valuable than a person who hears a hundred ideas but takes action on none of them.

Practice Makes Perfect

The more you practice what you are learning, the faster you will become competent and skilled in that area. The more you practice, the more confidence you will develop, the more rapidly you will overcome your feelings of inadequacy in that skill, and the faster you will master it. Once you add that skill to your mental toolbox, you will possess it for the rest of your career.

Resolve today, right now, to join the top 10 percent of people in your field. Determine who they are, what they earn, and what they do differently from you. Determine the special knowledge and skills they have developed and resolve to develop them yourself. Remember, anything that anyone has done, within reason, you can do as well. No one is better than you and no one is smarter than you. The very fact that the top people in your field were at one time not even in your field at all is proof that whatever they have achieved, you can achieve yourself if you simply set it as a goal and work at it long enough and hard enough. There are no limits.

⊞ BECOME AN EXPERT IN YOUR FIELD

1 Resolve today to join the top 10 percent of people in your field. Make a lifelong commitment to excellence.

2 Identify the key result areas of your job, the things you "absolutely, positively" have to do well to be successful in your field.

3 Identify your weakest key area and start a "do-it-to-yourself" project to become excellent in that area.

4 Determine the additional knowledge you will need to get to the top of your field and then develop a plan to acquire that knowledge.

5 Dedicate yourself to lifelong learning. Read, listen to audio programs, attend courses and seminars, and then put what you learn into action as quickly as you can.

12

Associate with the Right People

> Your outlook upon life, your estimate of yourself,
> your estimate of your value are largely colored by your
> environment. Your whole career will be modified, shaped,
> molded by your surroundings, by the character of the
> people with whom you come in contact every day.
> —ORISON SWETT MARDEN

Everything in life and business is *relationships*. Everything you accomplish or fail to accomplish will be bound up with other people in some way. Your ability to form the right relationships with the right people at every stage of your life and career will be the critical determinant of your success and achievement and will have an inordinate impact on how quickly you achieve your goals.

The more people you know, and who know you in a positive way, the more successful you will be at anything you attempt. One person, at the right time, in the right place, can open a door for you that can change your life and save you years of hard work.

No One Does It Alone

A key part of goal setting is for you to identify the people, groups, and organizations whose help you will require to achieve your goals. To accomplish goals of any kind, you will need the help of lots of people. Who are they?

There are three general categories of people whose help and cooperation you will require in the years ahead. These are the people in and around your business, your family and friends, and people in groups and organizations outside your business or social circle. You need to develop a strategy to work effectively with each group.

Your Key Business Relationships

Start with your business. Who are the most important people in your business life? What is your plan to develop higher quality relationships with them? Make a list of everyone who works inside and outside of your business—your boss, colleagues, coworkers, subordinates, and especially, your customers, suppliers, and vendors. Which of these people have the greater ability to help you or hurt you in the achievement of your business or career goals?

Sometimes I ask my audiences how many of the people present are in *customer service?* Only a few hands go up. I then point out that *everyone* is in the business of customer service, no matter what they call it or what they do.

Identify Your Customers

A customer can be defined as anyone who you depend upon for success and advancement in your job or business. A customer can also be defined as anyone who depends on you in any way. By this pair of definitions, almost everyone around you is a customer in some way.

For example, your boss is your *primary* customer at work. Your ability to satisfy your boss will have more of an impact on your future, your income, and your career than any other single skill you have. If you displease everyone else but your boss is delighted with you, you will be safe and secure in your job. If you please everyone inside and outside your company but your boss is unhappy with you, that problem alone can short-circuit your future.

Your Customer Service Strategy

One of the best strategies you can use is to make a list of everything that you believe that you have been hired to do. Answer the question, **Why am I on the payroll?** and write down everything you can think of. Then, take this list to your boss and ask your boss to organize this list in order of his or her priority. What is most important to your boss? What is second most important? What is third most important? And so on.

From that moment onward, discipline yourself to work on your boss's top task all day long. Make sure that whenever your boss sees you or talks to you, you are working on what he or she has told you is his or her top priority for you. This will do more to help you in your career than any other single decision you make.

Two Key Qualities for Promotability

In a survey reported in *Success Magazine* a few years ago, 104 chief executive officers were presented with twenty qualities of an ideal employee and asked to select the most important. Eight-six percent of the senior executives selected two qualities as being more important for career success and advancement than any others. First was the ability to set priorities, to separate the relevant from the irrelevant. Second was the ability to get the job done fast, to execute quickly.

Nothing will help you more in your career than to get the reputation for being the kind of person who gets the most important job done quickly and well.

Hard Work on the Wrong Task?

But here's the catch. Many people are working very hard at their jobs, but they are not working on what their boss considers to be the most important job. The sad fact is that if you do an unimportant job very well, this could *hurt* your career and even threaten your job.

As conditions change, keep the lines of communication open with your boss. Be sure that what you are doing today is still your boss's top priority. And then make a game of doing it *fast*. Nothing makes a boss happier than to have someone who gets the job done quickly. Be sure that you are that person.

Your Other Key Customers

Your coworkers, who also depend on your work, are your customers as well. Go to each one of them and ask them if there is anything that you can do to help them. Ask them if there is anything that you could do *more of or less of, anything that you could start or stop* doing that would help them do their jobs better.

The fact is that people think about themselves and their own jobs all day long. Anytime you offer to help people to do their jobs better or faster, they will be wide open to helping you later. The Law of Sowing and Reaping is not the Law of Reaping and Sowing. There is a particular order to this law. First you put in, and then you get out. First you sow, and then you reap.

You should look for every opportunity in your work to help people and to do nice things for others. Every honest effort you make to help other people will come back to you in some way, at some time, and often when you least expect it. The most popular people in every organization are those who are always willing to lend a helping hand.

The more the people next to you, above you, and below you like you and support you, the more you will get paid and the faster you will be promoted. Develop a reputation as a "go-giver," as well as being a go-getter.

Look for ways to be a valuable resource to the people around you and they will automatically look for ways to help you and support you when you most need it.

Be a Team Player

Perhaps the most important quality you can develop for long-term success in your business is that of being a good team player. In a multiyear study at Stanford University, researchers found that the ability to function well as part of a team was the most outwardly identifiable quality of a person who was marked for rapid advancement.

Team dynamics are very interesting. First of all, 20 percent of a team's members do 80 percent of the work. The other 80 percent contribute very little to the meetings and very seldom raise their hands or volunteer for anything. Your job is to be a member of the top 20 percent.

To be a good team player, always come prepared to every meeting. Sit opposite and in direct eye contact with the person who is running the meeting. Speak early and ask questions. Volunteer for assignments. And when you offer to do something, do it quickly and well so that it is clear who the *go-to* person is in the company.

The Most Important Ability Is Depend-Ability

You can create a positive, attractive force field of energy around you by developing a reputation for being the person who everyone can depend upon to get the job done. As a result, you will be given more and bigger jobs and both the authority and the rewards that go with those jobs.

Take time to get to know your subordinates and the people who are below you on the corporate ladder. Talk to them and ask them questions. Offer to help them if you can. Be especially kind and courteous with them. Go out of your way to compliment them and recognize them for their work. You will be amazed at the difference this makes in your career.

Invest in Relationship Building

In every organization, the person who knows the most people is usually the person who, like cream, rises to the top. Initially, it may seem that relationship building takes a lot of time. But it will pay for itself over and over again in the months and years ahead.

Outside of your business, you should get involved with your industry and with your industry associations. The most successful executives and sales professionals network regularly with other business people and in other business groups. They keep expanding their professional contacts and friendships.

Look at the business organizations in your community. Select one or two organizations that contain people it would be helpful for you to know in the years ahead. Attend their meetings and introduce yourself to them. Once you have decided that it would be useful for you to be a member of one of these organizations, join up and begin attending every meeting.

Network Professionally

Here is the best strategy of all for networking. Select an important committee within the organization and volunteer to work on that committee. Choose a committee that has other members on it that you would like to get to know over time. Choose a committee that is engaged in activities that will bring you into contact with other key people, both inside and outside the organization.

Once you join the committee, volunteer for assignments. Even though this work is unpaid, these activities give you an opportunity to work with and perform before other key people who can help you in your career sometime down the road.

Fully 85 percent of new positions are filled in America through word of mouth and personal contacts. The more people you know and work with in your industry, the more doors of opportunity will open for you when the time is right.

Think and Plan Long Term

Take a long-term perspective on your career. As you read your local newspapers, make a list of the top people in your community. Assemble the names, titles, and businesses of one hundred of the "players" in your city.

As you gather these names, write each of them a letter and send them something that is not business related. Send a copy of a small book, a poem, a newspaper clipping, or anything that might be of interest to them, based on what you have read about them.

Each time you see a reason to communicate with that person, drop him or her a note. Sometimes, I will make a phone call or write a letter to an executive who has just done something noteworthy that was reported in the business press. Often, I don't get through or make direct contact. But I continue to sow seeds, and sooner or later "what goes around, comes around." Eventually, I will meet key people socially or in business and they will remember that I dropped them a letter a week, a month, or even a year ago.

One of my most important clients remembered that I had written him a letter more than three years ago when I met him for the first time at a business convention. He said, "Aren't you the one that wrote me the letter about such and such?" That led to a conversation, a meeting, and many years of work with his organization.

Give of Yourself

A rule says, **"The more you give of yourself with no expectation of return, the more that will come back to you from the most unexpected sources."**

No effort that you make to expand your contacts will ever be completely lost. Like seeds, various contacts have different periods of germination. Some will yield results immediately. Some will not yield results for many months or even years. You must be prepared to be patient.

Dr. David McClelland of Harvard University researched the qualities and characteristics of high achievers in our society. What he found was that your choice of a "reference group," the people with whom you habitually associate, was more important in determining your success or failure than any other single factor. As Zig Ziglar says, "If you want to fly with the eagles, you can't continue to scratch with the turkeys."

Get Around the Right People

Make it a point to associate with the kind of people that you like, admire, respect, and want to be like sometime in the future. Associate with the kind of people that you look up to and would be proud to introduce to your friends and associates. The choice of a positive, goal-oriented reference group can do more to supercharge your career than any other factor.

Fly with the Eagles

There are countless examples where a person working at an average job, getting average results, and earning average pay has changed positions and gone to work with a highly progressive company. In a few weeks, that person's attitude has completely changed. By continued association with optimistic, results-oriented, go-ahead people, the previously average individual begins to perform at extraordinary levels. This is why almost every major change in your life will be associated with a change in the people you live or work with.

The Turning Points

At every turning point in your life, someone is usually standing there guiding you in one direction or another, opening or closing a door for you or helping you in some way. Baron de Rothschild once wrote, "Make no useless acquaintances." If you are really serious about being the best and moving to the top of your field, you cannot afford to spend your time with people who are going nowhere in their lives, no matter how nice they are. In this sense, you must be selfish with regard to yourself and your future ambitions. You must set high standards for your friends and associates and refuse to compromise.

Many people get into bad relationships and form useless friendships early in their careers. This is normal and natural. Nothing is wrong with making mistakes, especially if you are young and inexperienced. But it is unforgivable to continue to stay in a situation that is holding you back from realizing your full potential. And your choice of the people you associate with will have more of an impact on what you become than any other single factor.

Your Most Important Relationships

The third category of people whose help and cooperation you will require are your family and friends. As Benjamin Disraeli said, "No success in public life can compensate for failure in the home."

It is vital that you invest all the time and emotion necessary to build and maintain a high quality home life. When your family life is solid and secure, characterized by warm, loving relationships, you will do better in everything else in the outer world.

But if something goes wrong with your home life because of inattention or neglect, it will soon affect your results at work in a negative way. Problems at home distract your attention and drain your energy. They can often sabotage your career.

Deliberate Extremes

If you have to work very hard to get started in your field, be sure that you discuss and explain this clearly to the people in your family. Throughout your career you will be required to go to "deliberate extremes." You will have to work long hours and often many days without breaks or vacations in order to take advantage of an opportunity or to complete a project.

Be sure that you discuss these deliberate extremes in advance with the members of your family so that they understand what is happening and why you are doing it. Arrange to compensate them afterwards by taking time off or going away on family vacations. Keep your life in balance.

Become a Relationship Expert

Once you have decided upon the people, groups, and organizations whose help and cooperation you will need to achieve your goals, resolve to become a relationship expert. Always treat people with kindness, courtesy, and compassion. Practice the Golden Rule: Do unto others as you would have them do unto you.

Above all, the simplest strategy is to treat everyone you meet, at home or at work, like a "Million Dollar Customer." Treat other people as though they are the most important people in the world. Treat them as though they were capable of buying a million dollars' worth of your product or service.

As Emmet Fox once said, "If you must be rude, be rude to strangers, but save your company manners for your family."

Every day, in every way, look for ways to lighten the load and help other people to do their jobs better and live their lives more easily. This will build up a great reservoir of positive feeling toward you that will come back to benefit you year after year.

ASSOCIATE WITH THE RIGHT PEOPLE

1 Make a list of the most important people in your work and business life. Develop a plan to help each person in some way.

2 Make a list of the most important people in your personal life. Determine the kind of relationships you want to have with them and what you will have to do to achieve them.

3 Identify the groups and organizations in your community and your field that would be helpful to you to join. Phone today and arrange to attend the next meeting.

4 Make a list of the top people in your community or in your field, and make a plan to get to know them personally.

5 Look for every opportunity to expand your social and business circle. Send people letters, cards, faxes, and e-mails. Build bridges at every opportunity.

13

Make a Plan of Action

Thoroughness characterizes all successful men. Genius is
the art of taking infinite pains . . . All great achievement
has been characterized by extreme care, infinite
painstaking, even to the minutest detail.

—ELBERT HUBBARD

Your ability to set goals and make plans for their accomplishment is the "master skill" of success. No other skill will help you more in fulfilling your potential in achieving everything that you are able to accomplish.

All major accomplishments today are "multitask jobs." They consist of a series of steps that must be taken in a particular way in order to accomplish a result of any significance. Even something as simple as preparing a dish in the kitchen with a recipe is a multitask job. Your ability to master the skill of planning and completing multitask jobs will enable you to accomplish vastly more than most people and is critical to your success.

The purpose of planning is to enable you to turn your major definite purpose into a planned, multitask project with specific steps—a beginning, middle, and end—with clear deadlines and subdeadlines. Fortunately, this is a skill that you can learn and master with practice. This skill will make you one of the most effective and influential people in your business or organization, and the more you practice it, the better you will get at it.

Putting Your Plan Together

Fortunately, in the previous chapters you have identified and assembled all the ingredients necessary to create a plan for the achievement of one or more of your goals.

1. You now have a clear vision of your ideal end result, or goal, based on your *values*. You know what you want and why you want it.

2. You have written out your goals, organized them by priority, and selected your *major definite purpose.*

3. You have created *measures and standards* to track your progress. You have set both *deadlines and sub-deadlines* as targets to aim at.

4. You have identified the key *obstacles, difficulties, and constraints* that stand between you and your goal and organized them by priority.

5. You have identified the essential *knowledge and skills* that you will require to achieve your goal.

6. You have organized these competencies *by priority* and developed a plan to learn what you need to learn to accomplish what you have decided to accomplish.

7. You have identified the *people, groups, and organizations* whose help and cooperation you will require, both inside and outside your business. You have decided on the specific steps you are going to take to earn the support and assistance of these people in achieving your goals.

Throughout this process, you have written and taken notes so that you now possess the raw materials and tools for the creation of a plan of accomplishment.

Now you are ready to put it all together into a plan of action.

The Planning Process Is Essential

Some time ago, *Inc.* magazine conducted a study of fifty start-up companies. Half of these companies had spent several months and even more to develop complete business plans before they began operations. The other half of this group had started without detailed business plans and were simply reacting to events as they occurred in the day-to-day operations of the business.

Two to three years later, the researchers went back to determine the levels of success and profitability of these companies. What they found was quite interesting. The companies that had started operations with clear, written business plans, carefully thought through and detailed in every respect, were vastly more successful and profitable than those companies that had started spontaneously and had made things up as they went along.

The companies that had started on "the back of an envelope," where the founders were "too busy" to sit down and do the detailed work of strategic planning were almost all floundering. Many of them were already bankrupt and had gone out of business.

The Planning Process Was the Key

Here was the most interesting discovery: when researchers interviewed the business founders, they asked them, "How often do you refer to your strategic plan in the day-to-day operations of your business?"

In almost every case, the entrepreneurs and executives running the businesses had not looked at the strategic plan since it had been completed some months ago. Once it was done, they put it in a drawer and seldom revisited it until the following year, when they went through the strategic planning process again.

The most important finding was this: The plan itself was seldom referred to, but the process of thinking through the key elements of the business was vital to their success.

Planning Pays Off

General Dwight D. Eisenhower, after the successful invasion of Normandy in World War II, was asked about the detailed planning process that went into the invasion. He said, "The plans were useless, but the planning was indispensible."

It is the exercise of working through and discussing every key element of the business plan that is more important than any other step *at the beginning.* This is why Alec Mackenzie, the time management expert, said, "Action without planning is the cause of every failure."

An old military axiom says, "No plan ever survives first contact with the enemy." From the first day that you begin actual business operations, the situation will change so rapidly that your plan will become obsolete in many respects within a few days or even a few hours. But it is the process of planning that is most important. Scott McNealy of Sun Microsystems says, "In a start-up business, you have to throw out all assumptions every three weeks."

The Basis of All Great Achievements

All successful people work from written plans. The great human achievements of mankind, from the building of the Pyramids to the great industrial operations of the modern age, were proceeded by and accompanied by detailed plans, carefully designed and thought through from beginning to end—before they began.

In fact, every minute spent in planning saves ten minutes in execution. Every minute that you spend planning and thinking before you begin will save you time, money, and energy in getting the results you desire. This is why it is said that "Failing to plan is planning to fail."

Planning Saves Time and Expense

The number one reason for failure is *action without planning*. People who say that they are too busy to plan in advance must be prepared for unnecessary mistakes and great losses of time, money, and energy.

It is said that every new business start-up is a "race against time." From the first day, the company founders are scrambling to find a way to make more money than it costs to stay in business. If they figure out the "profit model" and begin generating revenues in excess of costs before the money runs out, the business can turn the corner and succeed. But if the money runs out before they figure out how to make more profits than losses, the company, like a plane in a dive, will crash and burn.

The Formula for Success

There is a six P formula for personal and business success: "Proper Prior Planning Prevents Poor Performance."

There are seven advantages to "Proper Prior Planning":

First, the planning process forces you to organize your thinking and identify all the key issues that must be dealt with if you are ultimately going to be successful.

Second, thinking through what you must do to accomplish your goals enables you to plan your actions carefully before you begin, thereby saving you enormous costs in time, people, and money.

Third, a good plan, thoroughly discussed and evaluated, enables you to identify flaws and errors that could prove fatal to your business later on. It enables you to ask "what if?" questions. For example, "What are the worst possible things that could happen if you were to take a particular course of action?"

The fourth benefit of proper prior planning is that it enables you to identify weaknesses in your plan and make provisions to compensate for those weaknesses. Often, you can identify a "fatal flaw" that would lead to the failure of the enterprise. This is only possible by going through the planning process.

Fifth, planning enables you to identify strengths and potential opportunities that you can take advantage of to increase the likelihood of success. Often, you will be unaware of your particular strengths or the opportunities that exist in the situation before you go through the planning process.

The sixth benefit of planning is that it enables you to focus your time and money and concentrate all of your resources on the one or two objectives that you must achieve to make an enterprise successful. In the absence of clear focus and concentration, you will tend to spread your energies over a wide area and accomplish very little.

The seventh benefit of proper planning is that it will inevitably save you hours, weeks, and months of confusion, mistakes, and losses of both money and energy.

You Can't Get There from Here

In many cases, as the result of careful planning and analysis, the decision makers will realize that it is not possible to achieve a particular goal with the time or resources available or under the existing circumstances. Sometimes, the very best business deals in your career are the ones that you don't get into in the first place.

I worked for a wealthy man some years ago who gave me a piece of advice I never forgot. He said, "It is always easier to get into something than it is to get out of it." He taught me that the time to do the careful thinking is before you commit resources and people, not afterwards.

The Vital Discipline

Planning is a discipline and a skill. It is both a habit and a competence. This means planning is a skill that you can master through repetition and practice, and it is much easier than you might think.

List Every Task and Activity

In its simplest form, a plan is a list of every activity that you will have to engage in, from the beginning to the end, to accomplish a specific goal or objective. To begin the process of planning, take a sheet of paper and make a list of everything that you can think of that you will have to do to achieve your goal.

As you think of new items, add them to the list. Continually revisit your list and revise the items and steps as you get more information. This list becomes your blueprint for the construction of your "dream house," your ideal goal or result.

Determine Priority and Sequence

Now organize your list by priority and sequence by determining which tasks or activities are more important than other tasks or activities. Organize the items from number one, the most important, all the way to the least important.

Organize your list by *sequence,* as well. In sequencing, you determine which activities need to be done before or after other activities. Often, one task cannot be accomplished until another task has been completed. Sometimes, the accomplishment of a single task can be the bottleneck or choke point in the entire process.

Identify the Limiting Factor

In planning, very often the success of a plan will be determined by the achievement of a particular goal or objective within the plan. It may be the completion of construction on a new office, store, or factory. It may be the date of delivery of the first finished product or service or the achievement of a particular level of sales. It could be the hiring of a key person for an essential job. The planning process helps you to identify the vital elements of a plan and focus more of your time and attention on the most important tasks and activities that must be accomplished before success is possible.

Expect Failure at First

No plan is perfect the first time it is created. Most plans to accomplish something new will fail over and over again at the beginning. This is to be expected. Your ability to accept feedback and make corrections to your plan of activity is vital to your success. Keep asking, What's working? and What's not working? Be more concerned with what's right rather than who's right.

Remember the old saying, "Back to the drawing board!" Whenever your plan doesn't work, relax, take a deep breath, and revisit it.

Focus on the Solution

When you have a problem, resolve to be *solution oriented*. Expect difficulties as a part of the process and resolve to respond to them effectively. If you are not achieving your goals on schedule, ask, What is the problem? What *else* is the problem? What are the solutions? What *else* is a solution? What can we do now? What is the next step?

It seems that when you begin work on the achievement of a new goal, you immediately experience setbacks, obstacles, difficulties, and temporary failure. This is to be expected. It is normal and natural. It takes tremendous effort to launch something new and make it successful. But this is the price that you have to pay to achieve the goals that you have set for yourself.

Think on Paper

Always think on paper. Be continually making lists and sublists of every step in every process. Keep updating and revising your plan, making it better and better until it is perfect.

Remember, planning is a skill. Because it is a skill, it is completely learnable. Your ability to think, plan, organize, and initiate action toward your goal will eventually put you in the top 10 percent of your field. But it takes time.

One of the ways that you can "think on paper" is to create a project-planning sheet for the accomplishment of a multitask goal. In this way, you create a visual image of your goal and the steps you need to take to achieve it. This can be very helpful in opening your eyes to the strengths and weaknesses of the planning process.

The Project-Planning Model

In project planning, you write the days, weeks, and months that you think the project will require to complete across the top of the page. If it is a twelve-month project or goal, you write the names of the twelve months, from this month forward. This gives you a timeline for the project.

Down the left-hand column, make a list of all the tasks that must be accomplished, in proper sequence, for you to achieve the ultimate goal. What will you need to start or do first? Second? And so on.

In the lower right-hand corner, write clearly what your final, ideal result will look like. The greater clarity you have about your desired goal, the easier it will be for you to reach it.

You can now use horizontal bars to indicate the amount of time necessary, from beginning to end, to complete a particular task. Some of these tasks can be done simultaneously and others will have to be done after something else is completed. Certain of these tasks are of high priority and others are of lower priority. But with a project planning sheet, you can now see your entire goal laid out in front of you with great clarity.

Assemble Your Team

Everyone who is responsible for carrying out a part of the plan should be involved in the planning process. It is quite common to make the mistake of assuming that a particular task can be completed quickly and easily. It is often a shock to find out that something that seems simple and easy is actually going to take several months from beginning to end. A time constraint on a critical part of your plan can force you to revise it completely.

One of my managers decided to send out a newsletter to all our customers on a new development in our business. He called our commercial designer and told her he needed it by the end of the week.

He was shocked to discover that a professionally written, designed, and produced newsletter would take six to eight weeks to print and mail and cost more than $2,000. The project was immediately scrapped.

When you start the planning process, your biggest concern should be accurately identifying every step necessary and the exact time required to accomplish every step in the plan. There is a time for optimism and there is a time for realism in making plans and achieving goals. You must be absolutely honest with yourself at every step of the planning process, and never trust to luck or hope that the laws of nature will be suspended temporarily on your behalf.

Identify the Potential Bottleneck

In the process of planning, usually one major problem must be solved before any other problems can be solved. Usually one major goal must be achieved before any of the other goals can be achieved or one critical element must be dealt with before any other part of the plan can be successful.

For example, many companies will start with every single detail in place except for a professional sales process to bring in revenues. The company will engage in a strategic planning process, rent or lease offices, buy furniture, set up the necessary computers and equipment to produce the product or service, hire the administrative and business staff, set up the books of account, and begin advertising. But a first-class selling process has not been installed, and within a few months, or even weeks, without sales revenues the company grinds to a halt. To a large extent, this is what happened to turn the dot-com explosion into a "dot-bomb" collapse.

Determine the Critical Results

What are the critical results that you must accomplish, at each step of the way, to achieve your final goal? How can you plan them, prioritize them, and assure that they are completed on schedule? What is your plan if things go wrong? What will you do if it takes much longer and costs much more to achieve your critical objectives on your way to the goal? What is your fallback plan? You may have heard the line, "A great life, like a great ship, should never be held by a single hope or a single rope."

Planning Is the Key to Success

The good news is that the very act of planning improves and streamlines the entire process of goal achievement. The more often and more carefully you plan before you begin, the better you will become at the planning process overall. The better you get at planning, the more ideas and opportunities you will attract to you to plan and achieve even bigger and better things.

Your ability to decide exactly what you want, write it down, make a plan, and then execute that plan is the key to personal effectiveness and high achievement. These are learnable skills that you can master. In no time at all, you can transform your life or business, double your sales or profitability, achieve your goals, and fulfill your true potential.

MAKE A PLAN OF ACTION

1 Make a list of everything that you can think of that you will have to do to achieve your goal. Leave nothing out.

2 Organize your list by priority; what is the most important task or activity? The second most important? And so on.

3 Organize your list by sequence: what must be done before something else can be done?

4 Determine how much time and money it will take to achieve your goal or complete your task. Do you have the time and resources necessary for success?

5 Revisit and revise your plan regularly, especially when you get new information or things are not going as you had expected. Be prepared to change if you need to.

14

Manage Your Time Well

Time slips through our hands like grains of sand,
never to return again. Those who use time wisely
are rewarded with rich, productive and satisfying lives.
—ROBIN SHARMA

To achieve all your goals and become everything you are capable of becoming, you must get your time under control. Psychologists generally agree that a "sense of control" is the key to feelings of happiness, confidence, power, and personal well-being. And a sense of control is only possible when you practice excellent time management skills.

The good news is that time management is a skill, and like any other skill, it is learnable. No matter how disorganized you have been in the past or how much you have tended to procrastinate or to get caught up in low-value activities, you can change. You can become one of the most efficient, effective, and productive people in your field by learning how others have gone from confusion to clarity and from frustration to focus. Through repetition and practice, you can become one of the most result-oriented people in your field.

Choices and Decisions

If the front side of the coin of success is the ability to set clear goals for yourself, then the flip side of the same coin is the ability to get yourself organized and work on your most valuable tasks, every minute of every day. Your choices and decisions have combined to create your entire life to this moment. To change or improve your life in any way, you have to make new choices and new decisions that are more in alignment with who you really are and what you really want.

The starting point of time management is for you to determine your goals, and then to organize your goals by priority and value. You need to be absolutely clear, at any given moment, exactly what is most important to you at that time.

At one moment, it could be a business, financial, or career goal. Later it could be a family or relationship goal. On still another occasion it could be a health or fitness goal. In each case, you must be like a sniper, rifling in on your highest priority at the moment, rather than a machine gunner, shooting off randomly by attempting to do too many things at the same time.

The Right Thing to Do

The metaphysician and philosopher Peter Ouspensky was once asked by a student, "How do I know what is the right thing for me to do?"

Ouspensky replied, "If you tell me your aim, I can tell you what is the right thing for you to do."

This is an important parable. The only way that you can determine what is right or wrong, more or less important, high or low priority is by first determining your aim or goal at that particular moment. From that point forward, you can divide all of your activities into "A" activities or "B" activities.

An "A" activity is something that moves you toward your goal, the faster and more directly the better. A "B" activity is an activity that does not move you toward a goal that is important to you.

The Role of Intelligence

In Gallup interviews of thousands of men and women to determine the root causes of success in life and work, the importance of "intelligence" was mentioned again and again. But when the researchers pressed for a definition of "intelligence," they received an interesting answer. Intelligence was not defined as a high IQ or good grades in school. Rather, intelligence was most commonly defined as a "way of acting."

In other words, if you act intelligently, you are intelligent. If you act unintelligently, you are unintelligent, irrespective of the grades you may have received or the degrees you have earned.

And what then, by definition, is an intelligent way of acting? An intelligent way of acting is anything that you do that is consistent with achieving the goals that you set for yourself. Each time that you do something that moves you closer toward something that you really want, you are acting intelligently. On the other hand, an unintelligent way of acting is doing things that are not moving you toward your goals, or even worse, are moving you away from your goals.

To put it bluntly, doing anything that does not help you achieve something that you have decided that you want for yourself is acting in a stupid manner. The world is full of people who are acting stupidly every day, and they are not even aware of what a negative effect this is having on their lives.

Determine Your Long-Term Goals

Time management begins with *clarity*. You take the time to sit down with a piece of paper and think through exactly what it is you want to accomplish in each area of your life. You decide upon your ultimate, long-term goals of financial success, family success, or personal health and fitness. Once you are clear about the targets you are aiming at, you then come back to the present and plan every minute and hour of every day so that you accomplish the very most that you possibly can with the time allocated to you.

Begin with a List

The basic tool of time management is a list, organized by priority, and used as a constant tool for personal management. The fact is that you can't manage time; you can only manage *yourself*. That is why time management requires self-discipline, self-control, and self-mastery. Time management requires that you make the best choices and decisions necessary to enhance the quality of your life and work. Then you follow through on your decisions.

You should plan your life with lists of long-term, medium-term, and short-term goals and projects. You should plan every month, in advance, with a list of the things you want to accomplish during that month. You should make a list of every step in each multitask job that you want to complete, and then organize that list by priority and sequence.

Use Advance Planning

Begin today to plan every week in advance, preferably the Sunday before the workweek begins. Plan every day in advance, preferably the night before.

When you make a list of everything you have to do the following day, your subconscious mind works on that list all night long. When you wake up in the morning, you will often have ideas and insights to help you accomplish the items on your list. By writing out your plans, you will activate the Law of Attraction. You will begin attracting into your life the people, opportunities, and resources that you need to achieve your goals and complete your tasks the very best way possible.

Separate the Urgent from the Important

In the process of managing your time, you must separate the urgent tasks from the important ones. Urgent tasks are determined by external pressures and requirements. You must do them immediately. Most people spend most of their days responding and reacting to urgent tasks in the form of telephone calls, interruptions, emergencies, and the demands of their boss and their customers.

Important tasks, on the other hand, are those that can contribute the very most to your long-term future. Some of these tasks may be planning, organizing, studying, researching your customers, and setting priorities before you begin.

Then there are tasks that are urgent but not important, such as a ringing telephone or a coworker who wants to chat. Because these activities take place during the workday, it is easy to confuse them with real work. The difference, however, is that they produce no results. No matter how many urgent but *un*important activities you engage in, you contribute nothing to your work or your company.

The fourth category of tasks includes those that are neither urgent nor important, like reading the paper at work or going for a long lunch. These activities are positively harmful to your career because they consume time that you could be using to get the results for which you are paid and upon which your future depends.

Consider the Consequences

The most important word in determining the value of a particular task or activity is *"consequences."* A task that is valuable and important is a task that has serious consequences for completion or noncompletion. The greater the possible consequences of a task or activity, the more important it is.

A task for which there are few if any consequences is by definition not particularly important. Your aim in personal management, therefore, is to spend more time doing more of those tasks that can have the greatest possible consequences on your life and work.

Apply the 80/20 Rule

Once you have prepared a list of tasks for the coming day, review your list and apply the 80/20 rule before you begin.

The 80/20 rule says that 20 percent of your activities will account for 80 percent of the value of all of your activities. If you have a list of ten items to complete, two of those items will be more valuable than the other eight items combined. Two of the ten tasks will have greater potential consequences than the other 80 percent.

Sometimes it will even be the "90/10 rule" that applies. Often one task on a list of ten items you have to do during the day will contain more value than everything else put together. This task, unfortunately, is usually the task that you will procrastinate on most readily.

Practice Creative Procrastination

Once you have identified your top 20 percent of tasks, you can then practice "creative procrastination" on the others.

Since you cannot do everything, you will have to procrastinate on something. The only question is, Which of your tasks are you going to procrastinate on?

The answer is simple. Procrastinate on the 80 percent of tasks that contribute very little to your desired goals and results. Focus your time and attention on completing those one or two jobs that can make the most difference.

Practice the ABCDE Method

Another method of setting priorities is the ABCDE Method. This method requires that you review your list of tasks, before you begin, and put an A, B, C, D, or E next to each one. The very act of performing this exercise and thinking through your tasks before you start work will dramatically increase your efficiency and effectiveness once you begin working.

An "A" task is something that is very important. It has serious consequences for completion or noncompletion. Whether you do it or don't do can have a major impact on your results and your success. You should always do your "A" tasks before anything else.

If you have more than one "A" task, organize them by priority, as A-1, A-2, A-3, and so on. Once you have completed this exercise, identify your A-1 task and focus all of your energies on starting and completing this job before you do anything else.

A "B" task is something that you should do. It has mild consequences for completion or noncompletion. For example, calling a friend, going for lunch with your coworkers or checking your e-mail would be a "B" task. Doing it or not doing it may cause some inconvenience, but the consequences for your life are minor.

A "C" task is a task that would be *nice* to do but it will have no consequences at all. Having another cup of coffee, chatting with a coworker, reading the paper or going shopping during the day are all "C" tasks. Whether you do them or not, they will have no consequences in your life or work at all.

The rule is this: Never do a "B" task when there is an "A" task left undone. Never do a "C" task when you have a "B" task left undone. Keep focused on your "A" tasks throughout the day.

A "D" task is something that you can *delegate* to someone else who works at a lower hourly rate than you do or than you want to earn. The rule is that you should delegate everything you possibly can so that you have more time to devote to your "A" tasks, the ones that determine most of your success and happiness in life and work.

An "E" task is something that you can *eliminate* altogether. These can be old activities that are no longer important in the achievement of your most important goals today. Much of what you do during the day or week can be eliminated with no consequences at all.

The Law of the Excluded Alternative

You are always free to choose. In this hour by hour and minute by minute choosing of what you will do and simultaneously what you will not do, your entire life is made. The Law of the Excluded Alternative says that Doing one thing means not doing something else.

Whenever you begin a task of any kind, you are consciously or unconsciously deciding not to do any other task that you could do at that moment. Your ability to choose wisely in terms of what you do first, what you do second, and what you do *not do at all* determines your entire life.

Choose the Most Valuable Task

Successful, highly paid people are usually no more intelligent or skilled than unsuccessful, lowly paid people. The major difference between them is that successful people are always working on tasks of high value. Unsuccessful people are always killing time on tasks of low value. And you are always free to choose. You are always free to choose what you do more of and what you do less of. Your choices ultimately determine everything that happens to you.

Practice Single-Handling on Each Task

Single handling is one of the most powerful time and personal management techniques of all. What this means is that, once you have selected your A-1 task, you start on that task and work on it with single-minded concentration until it is 100 percent complete. You discipline yourself to concentrate without diversion or distraction.

If you find yourself getting distracted or you feel tempted to take a break or procrastinate, you can motivate yourself by continually repeating, "Back to work! Back to work! Back to work!" You then renew your efforts to push the task through to completion.

Thomas Edison once wrote, "My success is due more to my ability to work continuously on one thing without stopping than to any other single quality." You should practice this principle as well.

Create Chunks of Time

Plan your day in advance and create thirty, sixty, and ninety-minute chunks of uninterrupted work time. These are time blocks when you can work without interruption or pause on your most important tasks. These chunks are essential for the accomplishment of any large, important task.

One way to create long periods of work time is to rise early and work nonstop, without interruption, on a major task, project, or proposal. Sometimes you can create chunks of time in the evenings or on the weekends. But the fact is, all important jobs, those with serious potential consequences, require large chunks of single-minded, concentrated time and energy.

Earl Nightingale once said, "Every great accomplishment of mankind has been preceded by an extended period, often over many years, of concentrated effort."

Keep Yourself on Track

Each day, before you begin and as you go through the day, there are five questions that you need to ask and answer, over and over again.

The first of these questions is, **Why am I on the payroll?** What exactly have you been hired to accomplish? If you were being questioned by your boss and your boss were to ask you, "Why do we pay you money around here?" what would be your answer?

The fact is that you have been hired to achieve specific results that have economic value to your organization. And of all your results, 20 percent of what you do contributes 80 percent of your value. You must be crystal clear about exactly why you are on the payroll and then focus your time and attention, all day long, on doing exactly those tasks that make the greatest difference to your business or organization.

Focus on High-Value Activities

The second question that you should ask yourself all day long is, **What are my highest value activities?** These are the activities that represent the highest and best use of your talents, skills, experience, and abilities as they relate to your company, career, and organization. What are they?

If you are not absolutely sure of the answers, go and ask your boss what he or she thinks your highest value activities might be. Whatever the answer, dedicate yourself to working on these specific tasks all day long.

Work on Your Key Result Areas

The third question you should ask all day long is, **What are my key result areas?** As we mentioned earlier, your key result areas are those tasks that you absolutely, positively must complete in an excellent fashion if you are to achieve the most important results required of your job. They largely determine your success or failure at work.

You should clearly identify each of these tasks and then focus on not only performing at your best in each of them but also at becoming better in each key result area every day. Remember, your weakest key skill sets the height at which you can use all your other skills. Don't allow yourself to be held back because of a weakness in one area, especially when you can learn anything you need to know to excel in that particular area.

Make a Difference!

The fourth question you should ask yourself throughout the day is this: **What can I and only I do, that if done well will make a real difference to my company?**

This is one of the best questions of all for keeping yourself focused and on track. What is it that you and only you can do that can make the greatest difference in your career? Again, if you are not sure of the answer, ask your boss. Sometimes, he or she will not have thought this through before you ask the question. Sometimes, he or she will not have thought about it at all.

But once both of you are in agreement on the one or two tasks you can do that will make more of a difference than anything else, you should focus all of your energies on performing those particular tasks quickly and well. This will do more to help you in your career than any other single decision you make.

The Most Important Question of All

The fifth question, and perhaps the best question in all of time management is this: **What is the most valuable use of my time, right now?** All techniques and methods of goal setting, personal planning, and time management are aimed at helping you to accurately answer this question, every minute of every day.

When you discipline yourself to ask and answer this question repeatedly, and you are sure that whatever you are doing is the answer to this question, you will start to accomplish two and three times as much as the people around you. You will become more and more productive. You will plow through more work of higher value and accomplish greater results than anyone around you. Discipline yourself to keep working on the most valuable use of your time, whatever it may be at the moment, and you will be successful.

Become Intensely Result Oriented

In the final analysis, the key to high productivity and performance is this: Dedicate yourself to getting better and better at the few tasks that you do that account for most of your results. Simultaneously, learn to delegate, outsource, and eliminate all those tasks and activities that contribute very little to your results and rewards.

As Goethe said, "The things that matter most must never be at the mercy of the things that matter least." Perhaps the best single word in time management is the word "no." Just say "No!" to any demand on your time that is not the most valuable use of your time at the moment.

Develop the Habits of Time Management

The good news is that time management is a skill and a discipline that you can learn with practice. One rule for success is, Develop good habits and make them your masters.

You can become excellent at time management with daily practice. Make a list of your tasks every day, before you begin. Organize your list by priority, separating the urgent from the important and using the 80/20 rule or the ABCDE Method. Choose your most important task and then begin working immediately on that task. Discipline yourself to concentrate single-mindedly on that one task or activity until it is 100 percent complete.

Each time you complete an important task, you will experience a burst of elation, enthusiasm, and heightened self-esteem. You will feel energized and stronger. You will feel happier and more in control of your life. You will feel on top of your work. You will be even more motivated to start, and complete, your next major task.

Whenever you find yourself slowing down or experiencing the urge to procrastinate or delay, repeat to yourself, "Do it now! Do it now! Do it now!" Develop a sense of urgency. Create a bias for action. Get started, get going, and work fast. Discipline yourself to select your most important task, launch into it immediately, and then stay with it until it is done. These time management practices are the keys to peak performance in every part of your life.

◈ MANAGE YOUR TIME WELL

1 Make a list of everything you would like to be, do, or have in the months and years ahead. Analyze your list and select those items that can have the greatest possible consequences on your life.

2 Make a list of everything you have to do the next day the evening before. Let your subconscious mind work on your list while you sleep.

3 Organize your list by priority using the 80/20 rule and the ABCDE Method. Separate the urgent from the nonurgent and the important from the nonimportant before you begin.

4 Select the most important task, the one with the greatest possible consequences for completion or noncompletion, and circle it, making it your A-1 job.

5 Begin immediately on your most important task, and then discipline yourself to concentrate singlemindedly on this one task until it is 100 percent complete.

15

Review Your Goals Daily

It is a psychological law that whatever we wish to accomplish we must impress on the subjective or subconscious mind.

—ORISON SWETT MARDEN

Sometimes I ask my audiences, "How many people here would like to double their incomes?" Not surprisingly, everyone raises his or her hand. I then go on to say, "Well, I have good news for you. Everybody here is going to double their income—guaranteed—if you *live* long enough!"

If your income increases at the rate of 3 percent to 4 percent per year, the average annual cost of living increase, you will double your income in about twenty years. But that is a long time to wait!

So the real question is not about doubling your income. The real question is, How fast can you do it?

Double the Speed of Goal Attainment

Many techniques can help you to achieve your personal and financial goals faster. In this chapter, I want to share with you a special method that has taken more people from rags to riches than any other single method ever discovered. It is simple, fast, effective, and guaranteed to work—if you will practice it.

Earlier, I said, "You become what you think about most of the time." This is the great truth that underlies all religion, philosophy, psychology, and success. As a teacher of mine, John Boyle, once said, "Whatever you can hold in your mind on a continuing basis, you can have." This is the key.

Positive Thinking versus Positive Knowing

Many people today talk about the importance of "positive thinking." Positive thinking is important, but it is not enough. Left undirected and uncontrolled, positive thinking can quickly degenerate into positive *wishing* and positive *hoping*. Instead of serving as an energy force for inspiration and higher achievement, positive thinking can become little more than a generally cheerful attitude toward life and whatever happens to you, positive or negative.

To be focused and effective in goal attainment, positive thinking must translate into "positive knowing." You must absolutely know and believe in the depths of your being that you are going to be successful at achieving a particular goal. You must proceed completely without doubt. You must be so resolute and determined, so convinced of your ultimate success, that nothing can stop you.

Program Your Subconscious Mind

Everything that you do to program your subconscious mind with this unshakeable conviction of success will help you achieve your goals faster. This method I am going to share with you can actually multiply your talents and abilities and greatly increase the speed at which you move from wherever you are to wherever you want to go.

One of the important mental laws is, Whatever is impressed, is expressed. Whatever you impress deeply into your subconscious mind will eventually be expressed in your external world. Your aim in mental programming is to impress your goals deeply into your subconscious mind so that they "lock in" and take on a power of their own. This method helps you to do that.

Systematic versus Random Goal Setting

For many years, I worked at my goals, writing them down once or twice a year and then reviewing them whenever I got a chance. Even this was enough to make an incredible difference in my life. Often, I would write down a list of goals for myself in January for the coming year. In December of that year, I would review my list and find that most of the goals had been accomplished, including some of the biggest and most unbelievable goals on the list.

I then learned the technique that changed my life. I discovered that if it is powerful for you to write down your goals once a year, it is even more powerful for you to write down your goals more often.

Some authors suggest that you write down and review your goals once a month, others once a week. What I learned was the power of writing and rewriting your goals *every single day*.

Write Down Your Goals Each Day

Here is the technique. Get a spiral notebook that you keep with you at all times. Each day, open up your notebook and write down a list of your ten to fifteen most important goals, without referring to your previous list. Do this every day, day after day. As you do this, several remarkable things will happen.

The first day you write down your list of goals, you will have to give it some thought and reflection. Most people have never made a list of their ten top goals in their entire lives.

The second day you write out your list, without reference to your previous list, it will be easier. However, your ten to fifteen goals will change, both in description and order of priority. Sometimes, a goal that you wrote one day will not appear the next day. It may even be forgotten and never reappear again. Or it may reappear later at a more appropriate time.

Each day that you write down your list of ten to fifteen goals, your definitions will become clearer and sharper. You will eventually find yourself writing down the same words every day. Your order of priority will also change as your life changes around you. But after about thirty days, you will find yourself writing and rewriting the same goals every day.

Your Life Takes Off

At about this time, something remarkable will happen in your life. It will take off! You will feel like a passenger in a jet hurtling down the runway. Your work and personal life will begin to improve dramatically. Your mind will sparkle with ideas and insights. You will start to attract people and re-sources into your life to help you to achieve your goals. You will start to make progress at a rapid rate, sometimes so fast that it will be a little scary. Everything will begin to change in a very positive way.

Over the years, I have spoken in twenty-three countries and addressed more than two million people. I have shared this "Ten-Goal Exercise" with hundreds of thousands of seminar participants. The exercise that I give them is a little simpler than the exercise that I am giving you here. Here it is.

I ask my audience members to make a list of ten goals that they want to accomplish in the coming year. I tell them to put the list away for twelve months and then open it up. When they open up the list after a year, it will be as though a magic trick has been performed. In almost every case, eight out of their ten goals will have been accomplished, sometimes in the most remarkable ways.

I have given this exercise all over the world, to people in every language and culture. In virtually every case, when I return to their cities and countries, people line up to talk to me, like in a wedding reception receiving line, and tell me story after story about how their lives have changed after writing down their ten goals a year or more ago.

Putting This Method to Work

In the exercise that we are discussing in this chapter, you will learn to get far greater and far faster results than those enjoyed by people who write their goals down only one time. Your results will double and triple and increase five and ten times as you use the same power of goal setting we have discussed earlier, but you will write your goals down every day.

You must follow some special rules to get the most out of this exercise. First, you must use the "Three *P* Formula." Your goals must be written and described in the positive, present, and personal tenses.

Activate Your Subconscious Mind

Your subconscious mind is only activated by affirmative statements phrased in the present tense. You therefore write down your goals as though you have *already* accomplished them. Instead of writing, "I will earn $50,000 in the next twelve months," you would write, "I earn $50,000 per year."

Your goals must be stated *positively* as well. Instead of saying, "I will quit smoking" or "I will lose a certain number of pounds," you would say, "I am a nonsmoker." Or, "I weigh X number of pounds."

Your command must be positive because your subconscious mind cannot process a negative command. It is only receptive to a positive, present tense statement.

The third "P" stands for *personal*. From now on, and for the rest of your life, write out every goal beginning with the word "I" followed by a verb of some kind. You are the only person in the universe who can use the word "I" in relation to yourself. When your subconscious mind receives a command that begins with the word "I," it is as though the factory floor receives a production order from the head office. It goes to work immediately to bring that goal into your reality.

For example, you would not say, "My goal is to earn $50,000 per year." Instead, you would say, "I earn $50,000 per year." Begin each of your goals with phrases such as, "I earn," "I weigh," "I achieve," "I win," "I drive such and such a car," "I live in such and such a home," "I climb such and such a mountain," and so on.

Set Deadlines on Your Goals

To add power to your daily written goals, put a deadline at the end of each goal.

For example, you might write, "I earn an average of $5,000 per month by December 31 (followed by a particular year)."

As we discussed in an earlier chapter, your mind loves deadlines and thrives on a "forcing system." Even if you do not know how the goal is going to be achieved, always give yourself a firm deadline. Remember, you can always change the deadline with new information. But be sure you have a deadline, like an exclamation point, after every goal.

How Badly Do You Want It?

This exercise of writing out your ten goals every single day is a test. The test is to determine how badly you really want to achieve these goals. Often you will write out a goal and then forget to write it down again. This simply means that you either don't really want to achieve that goal as much as something else or you don't really believe that that goal is achievable for you.

However, the more you can discipline yourself to write and rewrite your goals each day, the clearer you will become about what you *really* want and the more convinced you will become that it is possible for you.

Trust the Process

When you begin writing your goals, you may have no idea how they will be accomplished. This is not important. All that matters is that you write and rewrite them every day, in complete faith, knowing that every single time you write them down, you are impressing them deeper and deeper into your subconscious mind. At a certain point, you will begin to believe, with absolute conviction, that your goal is achievable.

Once your subconscious mind accepts your goals as commands from your conscious mind, it will start to make all your words and actions fit a pattern consistent with those goals. Your subconscious mind will start attracting people and circumstances into your life that can help you to achieve your goal.

Your Mental Computer Works Twenty-Four Hours per Day

Your subconscious mind works like a massive computer that is never turned off to help bring your goals into reality. Almost without your doing anything, your goals will begin to materialize in your life, sometimes in the most remarkable and unexpected ways.

Some years ago, I met with a businessman in Los Angeles who had an absolutely ridiculous idea. He wanted to raise many millions of dollars in investment capital to create an amusement park in Hawaii that would be composed of restaurants, displays, and exhibits from a variety of different countries from around the world. He was absolutely convinced that it would be a big attraction and that he could get the support and backing of all these different countries as long as he could raise the start-up money to launch the project. In my youth and inexperience, I gently told him that I thought his idea was a complete fantasy. The complexity and expense of such a massive undertaking was so vast for a person of his limited resources that it would be a complete waste of time. I thanked him for his offer of a job in putting this whole plan together and politely departed.

This was in the 1960s. The next thing I heard about this project was that the Walt Disney Corporation had embraced it in its entirety, called it the "Experimental Prototype Community of Tomorrow (EPCOT Center)," and had begun construction on it next to its Disney World in Orlando, Florida.

The amusement park and development has gone on to make hundreds of millions of dollars, year after year, and become one of the most popular tourist destinations in the world.

Activate All the Forces in the Universe

Here is the point. At that time, as a young man, I did not know that when you write down a goal, no matter how big or impossible it seems, you activate a series of forces in the universe that often make the impossible possible. I will explain this in great detail in the chapter on the "superconscious mind."

Whenever you write down a new goal of any kind, you may be skeptical and doubtful about the likelihood of accomplishing it. You may have the idea in your conscious mind, but you will have not yet developed the total belief and conviction that is possible for you. This is normal and natural. Don't let it stop you from using this method every day.

Just Do It!

All that is required to make this method work is for you to get a spiral notebook and then to discipline yourself each day to write down your ten goals in the positive, present, personal tense. That's all you need. In a week, a month, or a year, you will look around you and see that your whole life will have transformed in the most remarkable ways.

Even if you are skeptical about this method, it only requires about five minutes per day to try it. The good news is that I have never met a person, in more than twenty years, who has ever told me that this method does not work. It is quite the opposite. I get letters, phone calls, e-mails, and personal testimonials almost every day from people all over the country and all over the world whose lives have transformed so dramatically with this method as to be beyond belief!

Multiply Your Results

You can multiply the effectiveness of this method with a couple of additional techniques. First, after you have written down your goal in the positive, personal, present tense, write down at least three actions that you could take immediately to achieve that goal, also in the present, positive, personal tense.

For example, your goal could be to earn a certain amount of money. You could write, "I earn $50,000 over the next twelve months." You could then write, immediately underneath, "(1) I plan every day in advance, (2) I start in immediately on my most important tasks, (3) I concentrate single-mindedly on my most important task until it is complete."

Whatever your goal, you can easily think of three action steps that you can take immediately to achieve that goal. When you write down the action steps, you program them into your subconscious mind along with the goal. At a certain point, you will find yourself actually taking the steps that you wrote down, sometimes without even thinking about it. And each step you take will move you more rapidly toward your ultimate objective.

Use Three-by-Five-Inch Index Cards

Another way that you can increase the effectiveness of daily goal setting is by transferring your goals to three-by-five-inch index cards. Write one goal on each card in large letters.

Carry these cards with you at all times. Whenever you have a few spare moments, take out your index cards and review your goals, one by one.

Each of these goals should be written as a personal, positive, present tense affirmation. Someone once said, "I would rather a morning without breakfast than a morning without affirmations." Each time you use these cards, take a few moments, breath deeply and relax, and then review each of your goals, one at a time.

As you read the goal to yourself, imagine the goal as though it were already a reality. Actually see yourself at the goal, enjoying the goal, feeling the pleasure of having achieved the goal.

Alternately, as you read your index cards, imagine specific steps that you can take immediately to achieve that goal. You should actually imagine yourself taking those steps. Then relax, and go on to the next goal.

Ideally, you should review your goals on index cards at least twice per day. Remember to carry them around with you and review them during the day.

The Best Times for Mental Programming

Two times of the day are ideal for writing and rewriting your goals and for reading and reviewing your index cards. These are the last thing in the evening, before you go to bed, and the first thing in the morning, before you leave for work.

When you rewrite and review your goals in the evening, you program them into your subconscious mind. Your subconscious mind then has an opportunity to work on your goals all night long while you are sleeping. You will often arise with wonderful ideas for things to do or people to call to help you achieve your goals.

When you rewrite and review your goals in the morning before you start off your day, you set yourself up for positive thinking and positive acting all day long. Just as physical exercise in the morning warms up your body, reviewing your goals in the morning warms up your mind and prepares you to be at your very best throughout the day.

The result of rewriting and reviewing your goals each day, in the morning and evening, is that you will impress them ever more deeply into your subconscious mind. You will gradually move from positive *thinking* to positive *knowing*. You will develop a deep and unshakeable conviction that your goals are attainable and that it is only a matter of time before you achieve them, and you will be right.

⊞ REVIEW YOUR GOALS DAILY

1 Get a spiral notebook this very day and write down ten to fifteen goals that you would like to achieve in the foreseeable future.

2 Create a set of three-by-five-inch index cards with your goals written out in the positive, personal, present tense to carry with you wherever you go.

3 Each night before you go to sleep, visualize and imagine your life as it will be when you have achieved your goals.

4 Think of three things you could do to achieve each of your goals. Always think in terms of specific actions you could take.

5 Discipline yourself to rewrite your goals every day, without reviewing your previous list, until you become absolutely convinced that achieving your goals is inevitable.

16

Visualize Your Goals Continually

Cherish your visions and your dreams as they are
the children of your soul; the blueprints of your
ultimate achievements.

—NAPOLEON HILL

You possess and have available to you virtually unlimited mental powers. Many people are unaware of these powers and fail to use them for goal attainment. That is why their results are only average.

When you begin to tap into and unleash the power of your subconscious and superconscious minds, you will often achieve more in a year or two than most people achieve in a lifetime. You will start moving more rapidly toward your goals than you can currently imagine.

Your Most Powerful Faculty

Your ability to visualize is perhaps the most powerful faculty that you possess. All improvement in your life begins with an improvement in your mental pictures. You are where you are and what you are today largely because of the mental pictures that you hold in your conscious mind at the present time. As you change your mental pictures on the *inside*, your world on the *outside* will begin to change to correspond to those pictures.

Visualization activates the Law of Attraction, which draws into your life the people, circumstances, and resources that you need to achieve your goals.

Visualization also activates the Law of Correspondence, which says, "As within, so without." As you change your mental pictures on the inside, your world on the outside, like a mirror, begins to change. Just as you become what you think about most of the time, you become what you visualize most of the time as well.

Wayne Dyer says, "You will *see* it when you *believe* it." Jim Cathcart says, "The person you see is the person you will be." Dennis Waitley says that your mental images are "Your previews of your life's coming attractions."

Albert Einstein said, "Imagination is more important than facts." Napoleon Bonaparte said, "Imagination rules the world." Napoleon Hill said, "Whatever the mind of man can conceive and believe, it can achieve."

The Importance of Vision

The most common characteristic of leaders at all levels, throughout the ages, is vision. This means that they can visualize and imagine an ideal future, well in advance of its becoming a reality. Just as Walt Disney clearly saw a happy, clean, family-oriented amusement park many years before Disneyland was built, everything worthwhile in your life begins with a mental picture of some kind.

As it happens, you are always visualizing something, one way or another. Every time you think of someone or something, remember a past event, imagine an upcoming event, or even daydream, you are *visualizing*. It is essential that you learn to manage and control this visualizing capability of your mind and focus it, like a laser beam, in the direction of achieving the goals that are most important to you.

See the Success You Desire

Successful people are those who visualize the kind of success they want to enjoy *in advance*. Prior to every new experience, the successful person visualizes previous success experiences that are similar to the upcoming event. A successful salesperson will visualize and remember successful sales presentations. A successful trial lawyer will visualize and remember his performance in court during a successful trial. A successful doctor or surgeon will visualize and remember her successful treatment of a patient in the past.

Unsuccessful people, on the other hand, also use visualization but to their detriment. Unsuccessful people, prior to a new event, recall, reflect upon, and visualize their previous "failure experiences." They think about the last time they failed or did poorly in this area and they imagine failing again. As a result, when they go into the new experience, their subconscious minds have been preprogrammed for failure rather than success.

Feed Your Mind with Exciting Images

Your performance on the outside is always consistent with your self-image on the inside. Your self-image is made up of the mental pictures that you feed into your mind prior to any event. And the good news is that you have complete control over your mental pictures for good or for ill. You can choose to feed your mind with positive, exciting success images, or you can, by default, allow yourself to be preoccupied by failure images. The choice is up to you.

Almost everything that you have achieved in life, or failed to achieve, is the result of the use or misuse of visualization. If you look back, you will find that almost everything you visualized positively eventually came true for you. You visualized completing school, and you did it. You visualized getting your first car, and you got it. You visualized your first romance or relationship, and you met the right person. You visualized taking a trip, getting a job, finding an apartment, or purchasing certain clothes, and all these events came true for you.

Take Control of Your Mental Pictures

You have been using the power of visualization continuously throughout your life. But the problem is that most people use visualization in a random and haphazard way, sometimes to help themselves and sometimes to hurt themselves.

Your goal should be to take complete control of the visualization process and be sure that your mind and mental images are focused continually on what you want to have and the person that you want to be.

The Indispensable Man

George Washington, the first president of the United States, considered by most historians to be the "indispensable man" at the founding of the American Republic, started his life in humble circumstances. He was born in a small house and raised with few advantages. But he was ambitious and at an early age he decided that he had to mold and shape his character and personality so that he could become the kind of person who would be accepted and successful in society.

The guiding influence of his young life became a book with 130 rules for manners and deportment. He read this book over and over again and eventually committed it to memory. Thereafter, he practiced the very best courtesy and manners in his every interaction with other people. By the time he became a powerful figure in the American Revolution, he was described as one of the most courtly and gentlemanly men in the American colonies.

Develop Your Own Character

Benjamin Franklin, America's first millionaire, a founding father, and a remarkable statesman, diplomat, and inventor, started as a penniless boy in Philadelphia apprenticed to a small printing company. He was outspoken and argumentative and often made enemies who then contrived to hurt his chances and hold him back.

At a certain point in his young life, as Benjamin Franklin reveals in his autobiography, he realized that his personality was in great danger of hurting his chances for long-term success in early American society. He therefore decided to develop within himself a series of key virtues, such as sincerity, humility, temperance, discipline, and honesty, that he felt he would have to possess if he wanted to achieve his full potential.

For many years, week after week, both Washington and Franklin practiced visualization. They thought of a characteristic or quality that they wanted to embody. They visualized and imagined themselves as possessing that quality. In every interaction with other people, they referred to this "inner mirror" to see how they should behave and then carried themselves in a manner consistent with that ideal inner picture. Over time, these mental images became so deeply impressed on their subconscious minds that the mannerisms and the person became one.

You Are What You Can Be

Piero Ferucci, in his book *What We May Be,* explains how you can develop any quality you desire by dwelling upon that quality continually and imagining that you have it already. Read about the quality you desire. Learn about it. And especially, imagine yourself practicing that quality whenever it is needed.

Aristotle wrote that the very best way to develop a virtue, if you currently lack it, is to imagine and to behave in every respect as though you already had the virtue whenever that virtue is called for. See and think about yourself as you can be, not just as you might be today. Gradually, you will become that new person.

Change Your Mental Pictures

In essence, you control the molding and shaping of your own personality and character by the mental images that you dwell upon hour by hour and minute by minute. By changing your mental images, you change the way you think, feel, and act. You change the way that you treat other people and the way they respond to you. You change your performance and your results. You can actually remake yourself in the image of the very best person that you can imagine yourself becoming. This is all part of the constructive use of visualization.

Perform at Your Best

In professional athletics, there is a training method called "mental rehearsal." Top athletes in every field mentally rehearse their events before they go into active competition. They see themselves performing at their best prior to every event. For many days and hours prior to a major competition, they visualize themselves performing successfully, over and over again.

They continuously recall their "personal bests" in previous competitions and replay this personal best like a "movie of the mind" in their own mental screening room. They see themselves doing well over and over and feel the joy and satisfaction that accompany a peak performance. They become excited and happy about doing just as well in the upcoming competition. And when the competition begins, as far as they are concerned, they have already *won*.

Relax Deeply and See the Desired Result

Figure skaters, for example, play the music to their skating routines over and over again while they sit, deeply relaxed, with their eyes closed, imagining themselves skating on the ice. One of the benefits of skating in their minds is that they never fall or make a mistake. They see themselves skating their routines perfectly, over and over again, before they actually go onto the ice. By that time, their subconscious minds have been trained to take them through their routines smoothly and gracefully.

Your physical body has no mind of its own. The slightest movement of your fingers or toes is controlled by your central computer, your brain. It is your mind that sends impulses of nerve energy down your spine and throughout your body to your muscles to coordinate your physical activities. When you visualize, you actually train your master computer. You program your mind with the performance that you want your body to carry out.

Four Parts of Visualization

There are four parts of visualization that you can learn and practice to assure that you use this incredible power to its best advantage all the days of your life.

How Often?

The first aspect of visualization is *frequency,* the number of times that you visualize a particular goal as achieved or yourself performing in an excellent way in a particular event or circumstance. The more frequently you repeat a clear mental picture of your very best performance or result, the more rapidly it will be accepted by your subconscious mind and the more readily it will appear as part of your reality.

How Long?

The second element of visualization is the *duration* of the mental image, the length of time that you can hold the picture in your mind each time you replay it. When you deeply relax, you can often hold a mental picture of yourself performing at your best for several seconds and even several minutes. The longer you can hold your mental picture, the more deeply it will be impressed into your subconscious mind and the more rapidly it will express itself in your subsequent performance.

How Clearly?

The third element of visualization is *vividness*. There is a direct relationship between how clearly you can see your desired goal or result in your mind and how quickly it comes into your reality. This element of visualization is what explains the powers of the Law of Attraction and the Law of Correspondence. The vividness of your desire directly determines how quickly it materializes in the world around you.

Here is an interesting point. When you set a new goal for yourself, your image or picture of this goal will usually be vague and fuzzy. You may have no idea at all what the successful goal will look like. But the more often you write it, review it, and repeat it mentally, the clearer it becomes for you. Eventually, it will become crystal clear. At that point, the goal will suddenly appear in your world, exactly as you imagined it.

How Intensely?

The fourth element of visualization is *intensity,* the amount of emotion that you attach to your visual image. In reality, this is the most important and powerful part of the visualization process. Sometimes, if your emotion is intense enough and your visual image is clear enough, your goal will immediately come true.

Nature Is Neutral

Of course, the elements of frequency, duration, vividness, and intensity can help you or hurt you. Like nature, the power of visualization is neutral. Like a two-edged sword, it can cut in either direction. It can either make you a success or make you a failure. Visualization brings you whatever you vividly and intensely imagine, whether good or bad.

For example, worry is a form of negative goal setting. It is the process of thinking about, imagining, and visualizing, with fear and anxiety, exactly what you *don't* want to happen. When you worry, you are using visualization in a negative way. Exactly those problems that you don't want will be attracted into your life. In Job 3:25, Job says, "The thing which I greatly feared has come upon me." This refers to the unhappy consequences of negative visualization. You must be very careful how you use the visualizing power.

Design Your Dream Home

When my wife and I got married, we had very little money, and after I started my own business, what little we had quickly ran out. Nonetheless, like all couples, we talked about someday having our "dream home." We fantasized about living in the perfect home for ourselves and our family. Eventually, we decided to put the powers of visualization to work for us in the acquisition of our dream home.

Although we were living in a rented house at the time and had very little money, we subscribed to several magazines that described beautiful homes for sale around the country. We read *Better Homes and Gardens* and *Architectural Digest*. On the weekends, we went to open houses in the best neighborhoods in town. We walked through the rooms of beautiful, expensive homes and imagined living in those surroundings.

In complete faith that the process would eventually work, we created a scrapbook made up of pictures and descriptions of beautiful homes. Over time, we created a list of forty-two items that we wanted to have in our ideal house.

Meanwhile, I kept working at my job, building my business, increasing our income, and adding to our savings. Within a year of starting this process, we had moved from a rented house into a beautiful home that we had purchased in a lovely neighborhood. It was ideal in many respects, but we knew in our hearts that it was not yet our "dream house."

Patience Is Essential

A year and a half later, we moved again, this time to San Diego. After a month spent looking at dozens of homes for sale all over the city, we walked into a home that had just been listed two days before and knew immediately that we had found our dream house. We looked at each other without speaking and looked around at the house. We were both in perfect agreement.

It took two months of negotiation to finalize the purchase price and five more months to arrange the financing, but right on schedule, we took possession of our dream house, and we have lived there ever since. And it turned out to have forty-one of the forty-two items that we had listed for our perfect home.

Think Thin

Most people want to be physically fit and trim. Psychologists will tell you that this is only possible when you "think thin." One way you can create this mental image of thinness is to take a photo of a person who has the kind of body you would like to have, cut off the head, and put your photo there instead. Put this picture on your refrigerator. Make multiple copies of it if you can and put them all over your house.

Every time you look at a picture of yourself with a beautiful body, your subconscious mind will register it. Eventually, you will find yourself eating less and exercising more. Your outer reality will soon correspond to your inner picture.

Find Your Soul Mate

Often single people ask me how they can find their "soul mate." I ask them if they have made up a list and created a picture of what their soul mate will look like. They are always surprised and sometimes insulted. They say, "I will know the person when I meet him (or her)."

But that's not the way it works. *Casualness brings casualties.* If you don't have a clear idea of what you want, you end up getting something else. I advise these single people to sit down and write out a complete description of their ideal person, including every single quality and characteristic that they would like their soul mate to have. I tell them to be clear about age, temperament, personality, interests, values, background, sense of humor, level of ambition, and so on.

It is absolutely amazing what happens. A good friend of mine, a graduate of one of my three-day seminars, did this immediately after the program. Ten months later, he met a woman who fit his written description perfectly. They got married shortly thereafter, had two beautiful children, and have been happy from the first moment they met.

If you are single, you should give this technique a try. You might be happily surprised at what happens.

As Within, So Without

In every area of your life, you can use visualization to make it better. Earlier in this book, I talked about the use of "idealization." This process involves creating an ideal picture of what you would like your life to look like sometime in the future. Idealizing is just another version of visualizing. Remember, you can't hit a target that you can't see. But if you are absolutely clear about what you want, you will eventually achieve it.

The Best Times to Practice

As with goal setting, the two best times to visualize are late in the evening and early in the morning. When you visualize your goals as if they were already achieved before you go to sleep, your subconscious mind accepts them at a deeper level. It then adjusts your words and actions during the day so that you do and say more and more of what will make your goals into realities.

Another time to visualize is first thing in the morning. Clear mental images of what you want to accomplish during the day will make it far more likely that you will achieve those results, exactly as you imagined and on schedule.

The Beginning of All Improvement

To repeat, all improvement in your life starts with an improvement in your mental pictures. Start today to flood your mind with pictures of the person you want to be, the life you want to live, and the goals you want to achieve. Cut out pictures from magazines and newspapers that are consistent with your goals and desires. Post them everywhere. Review them regularly. Discuss them often. Imagine them continually.

Make your life an ongoing process of positive visualization, continually imagining and "visioneering" your ideal goals and your perfect future. This can do more to help you to step on the accelerator of your own potential than any other exercise you engage in.

▓ | VISUALIZE YOUR GOALS CONTINUALLY

1 Project forward and imagine that your life was perfect in every respect. What would it look like? Whatever your answer, imagine this picture regularly.

2 Cut out pictures of the things you would like to have and the person you would like to be in the future. Look at these pictures and think about what you could do to make them into realities.

3 Use mental rehearsal before every event of importance. See yourself in your mind's eye as performing at your very best in everything you do or attempt.

4 Continually feed your mind with clear, exciting, emotional pictures. Remember, your imagination is your preview of life's coming attractions.

5 Design your own dream house, dream business, or dream career. Write down every ingredient it would have if it were perfect in every respect. Visualize this as a reality every day.

Make the process of visualization a regular part of your life. Invest the time regularly to create exciting mental pictures of yourself and your life exactly as you want them to be. Then, have complete faith that your pictures will materialize exactly when you are ready.

17

Activate Your Superconscious Mind

The subjective mind is entirely under the control of the objective mind. With the utmost fidelity, it works to its final consequences whatever the subjective mind impresses upon it.

—THOMAS TROWARD

Imagine that you had just moved into a new house and the previous owner, just before leaving, took you aside privately. He explained that there was a special room in the basement that contained a most amazing computer. You could program any goal or question into that computer and it would give you exactly the right answer for you at exactly the right time. It worked every single time. And every answer would turn out to be perfectly correct. Imagine what an incredible difference this could make in your life!

The fact is that you do have such a computer. It is available and accessible to you at any time. It is called your "superconscious mind." It is the most powerful faculty ever discovered in all of human history, and you can tap into it any time you want.

Throughout this book, I have repeated that "You become what you think about most of the time" and "Whatever you can hold in your mind on a continuing basis, you can have." In addition, we discussed the Laws of Attraction and Correspondence and the importance of absolute clarity in determining exactly what you want to be, have, and do. In every case, I was referring indirectly to the power of the super-conscious mind.

The Secret of the Ages

The superconscious mind has been known about and discussed for thousands of years, throughout all of human history. For most of this time, it was the secret knowledge of the mystics and sages. Access to it was guarded and only taught after many years of loyal study to the devotees of the mystery schools of the ancient world. Only in the last one hundred years has the knowledge of the superconscious mind become more generally available and then only to a few people.

Three Minds in One

Sigmund Freud, the founder of psychotherapy, wrote about the three minds, the "ego," "id," and "superego" in 1895 and based much of his work upon these three different elements of perception.

The ego was described as the "I am," the part of the mind that is alert and aware, that deals with the external world, that analyzes, decides, and takes action. We call this the *conscious* mind.

The id of Sigmund Freud is the unconscious part of the mind or what we call the *subconscious* mind. This is the vast storehouse of memories and feelings where all of our previous thoughts, decisions, and experiences are gathered and which functions automatically both to operate our physical bodies and to keep our thoughts and feelings consistent with our past experiences.

What Sigmund Freud called the superego, the third dimension of thought, was referred to as the "oversoul" by

Ralph Waldo Emerson. Alfred Adler, a student of Freud, called it the "collective unconscious," and Carl Jung, who broke away from Freud, called it the "Supra Conscious." Napoleon Hill referred to it as "Infinite Intelligence," and reported that virtually all of the most successful people in America used it continually throughout their careers and credited it with their most important breakthroughs and accomplishments.

Roberto Assagioli, the Italian psychologist, and others refer to it as the "superconscious mind" or "God Mind." No matter what you call it, it is a great universal power that you can access at any time to achieve any goal that you really want as long as you desire it intensely—long enough and hard enough.

The Source of All Breakthroughs

All important breakthroughs in all fields throughout history have been the result of superconscious functioning. Whenever you have suddenly originated a great idea or insight that solved a problem or resolved a dilemma, you have had a superconscious experience. Great scientific breakthroughs, like the discovery of DNA or the idea of combining ceramics with electricity that led to the discovery of super conductivity, were superconscious in origin.

The great musicians tapped into and used their superconscious minds repeatedly in the creation of their compositions. Mozart could see an entire opera in his mind, note perfect, before he began writing. He would then transcribe the opera from his mental picture, without a single mistake, the very first time, ready to be played in public without revision. Nothing like this had ever been seen or experienced in all the history of music.

Beethoven created his greatest compositions after he went deaf. He could see and hear them in his mind before writing them down on paper. Stephen Hawking, the physicist, is so crippled with Lou Gehrig's disease that he needs a special computer to produce one letter at a time. Nonetheless, by using his superconscious mind, he has become one of the best-selling authors in the world with his book, *A Brief History of Time.*

The Greatest Inventor of All Time

Thomas Edison patented 1,093 devices at the U.S. Patent Office, almost all of which were turned into commercial products during his lifetime. At his death in 1931, fully one-sixth of the American workforce was employed in the manufacture and distribution of Thomas Edison–invented products.

Edison used his superconscious mind continually throughout his entire career to solve seemingly unsolvable problems and achieve historic breakthroughs in electricity, motion pictures, sound recording and transmission, and hundreds of other areas. He would take regular naps during the day to access his superconscious mind for insights that led to his numerous inventions.

The Great Law

Whenever you see a great and inspiring work of art, read a piece of classic literature or a beautiful poem, hear an extraordinary piece of music, or see a remarkable building or structure, you are witnessing the result of the superconscious mind in action.

The Law of Superconscious Activity, perhaps the most important mental law ever discovered, is this: **Any thought,** plan, goal, or idea held continuously in the conscious mind must inevitably be brought into reality by the superconscious mind.

Just think! Anything that you really want to be, have, or do is possible for you. If you can be absolutely clear about what it is and then access your superconscious mind on a regular basis, you will eventually achieve it. The only limits on what your superconscious mind can do for you are the limits that you place on your own mind and imagination.

The Right Operating Conditions

Your superconscious mind operates best when you are in a mental state of calm, confident, relaxed expectation. Whenever you practice relaxation in solitude, completely letting go of all your cares and sitting quietly or communing with nature, your superconscious mind begins to function.

Whenever you "go into the silence" and listen to the still, small voice within you, you begin to hear the whisperings of your superconscious mind.

Your *intuition* is the equivalent of that supercomputer in the basement of your new home. This is your connection and your contact with the superconscious mind. Sometimes your intuition will speak to you so loudly in the silence that the idea or insight it brings you will change your entire life.

The Greek scientist Archimedes had a superconscious flash of inspiration about the displacement of objects while sitting in his bath. He became so excited that he leaped from the bath and ran naked through the streets of Athens shouting "Eureka!" ("I have found it!"). This is how you often feel when you have a great idea or insight that solves a problem or moves you toward your goal.

Activating Your Superconscious

Your superconscious mind is stimulated by clear, written, specific goals, intensely desired, visualized regularly, and constantly worked toward.

Whenever you relax, visualize, and emotionalize a specific result that you intensely desire, you stimulate your superconscious mind into giving you ideas and energy for goal attainment.

Sometimes, a superconscious inspiration can so energize and excite you that you will be unable to sleep or think about anything else. In that case, you should sit down and write out every idea and detail that comes to you. This will often free up your mind and enable you to go back to sleep.

Serendipity and Synchronicity

The superconscious mind explains two phenomena that you experience regularly throughout your life, *serendipity* and *synchronicity*. The more you use your superconscious mind, the more often you will enjoy these two wonderful experiences.

Serendipity is the process of making happy discoveries along the road of life. Whenever you have a clear goal that you visualize continually and that you are working toward each day, happy, unexpected events and experiences occur in your life, each of which seems to help you to achieve your goals even faster.

You might come across an article in a magazine or someone will mention something to you that you didn't know before. You might even flip to a program on television that has exactly the idea or insight you need to solve a particular problem or answer a key question. You will often have a setback or temporary failure that turns out to be exactly the right thing to happen to you at that moment.

Look for the Good

The interesting point is that if you look for something good in every situation, you will always seem to find it. The very attitude of expecting good things to happen to you seems to trigger their occurrence over and over again. If you calmly and confidently believe in the magic of serendipity, no matter what happens, you will have repeated serendipitous experiences that will help you to achieve your *real* goals in life.

Events Connected by Meaning

The second phenomenon that you will experience regularly is called "synchronicity." This is different from the Law of Cause and Effect, the iron law of the universe, in a special way. The Law of Cause and Effect says that everything happens for a specific reason and that there is a traceable cause for every effect.

With synchronicity, however, the only relationship between two simultaneous events is the *meaning* that you give to them based on the goals that you have in different areas of your life.

Here is an example. You set a goal to double your income. But the following week, you either quit or get fired, completely unexpectedly. This initially looks like a real setback. But the next day, a friend asks you if you have ever thought of working in a particular field. As it happens, you have read several articles about that field over the past year and you have thought of getting into it, but you did not know how to go about it. You decide to investigate further, identify a growing company, interview for a job, start work, and one year later you find yourself earning twice as much as you were at your previous job and enjoying it more.

You will notice that there was no *direct* cause-and-effect relationship between these separate events. They seemed to be disconnected in time and space. But they have one thing in common. They helped you to achieve the real goal that you had set for yourself, to double your income.

Two Ways to Stimulate Your Superconscious Mind

There are two ways for you to stimulate your superconscious mind into action. The first is for you to concentrate and work intensely on achieving your goal. Throw your whole heart into what you are doing. Think about it, talk about it, write it, rewrite it, and review it every single day. Do everything that you can possibly think of that can help you to attain that goal.

When you dedicate yourself to continuous, determined forward action toward the accomplishment of your goal, all sorts of serendipitous and synchronous events will happen to you and for you. People will emerge from unexpected places to help you. You will receive phone calls and offers of assistance. You will come across ideas and information that you would not have recognized before. You will have ideas and insights that move you even faster toward your goal.

The second way to stimulate your superconscious mind is to relax completely and get your mind busy elsewhere. For example, when you go on vacation, you often become so busy with other activities that you don't think about your goals or problems at all. It seems that the more you can completely relax and let go, both mentally and physically, the more rapidly your superconscious mind will click into action and begin giving you the ideas and insights that you need. In other words, the harder that you "don't try," the faster your superconscious mind will work for you.

You should try both methods on every goal. First, work with single-minded concentration on the goal. Commit 100 percent of your energies to solving the problem. Then, if you have still not experienced the breakthrough you desire, get your mind busy elsewhere. Take some time off. Go on vacation. Engage in physical exercise or go to a movie. Forget about it completely for a while. Then, at exactly the right time, your superconscious mind will function and the answer will appear.

Exactly the Right Answer

Your superconscious mind will bring you the exact answer you need, at exactly the right time for you. Therefore, when you receive a superconscious inspiration, you should take action *immediately*. Don't delay. This is often *time-dated* information. If you get an inner urge to take an action or make a phone call, move on it quickly. If you have a hunch about something, follow up on it. It seems that the very act of moving on a superconscious flash will trigger additional superconscious insights and inspirations that will help you.

Three Special Qualities

A superconscious idea or solution has three qualities:

- First, it will answer every aspect of the problem or give you everything you need to achieve your goal. The answer will be complete in every respect.

- Second, it will be a "blinding flash of the obvious." A superconscious inspiration will feel natural, easy, and perfectly suitable to the situation.

- Third, a superconscious solution will give you a burst of happiness and excitement, even *exhilaration*. It will be one of those shining moments that you remember for a long time.

Whenever you get a superconscious solution, it will be accompanied by the energy, enthusiasm, and motivation you need to take action immediately. You will have an irresistible desire to implement the solution right now. You will want to stop everything else you are doing to take action. And you will always be right.

Trust Is the Key Requirement

Your superconscious mind is the most powerful faculty you have. It is available and accessible to you at all times. You "dial in" to your superconscious mind by being absolutely clear about what you want and then by calmly and confidently trusting that exactly the answer you need will come to you at exactly the time you are ready for it.

The more you relax and trust in this great power, the better and faster it will function. It has been said that "Men and women begin to become great when they begin to listen to their inner voices." When you make a regular habit of listening to your intuition and trusting your inner voice, you will probably never make another mistake. By tapping into your superconscious mind, you begin to bring your whole life into harmony with this great universal power. You will achieve goal after goal and move forward faster and faster in everything you do. You will feel as though you are plugged into some kind of cosmic energy source that enables you to accomplish vastly more, and with much less effort, than ever before.

Think back over your life and recall the times when your superconscious mind has worked for you. In the past, these experiences were random and haphazard. But by developing absolute clarity about your goals and by reviewing and visualizing them regularly, you can make this superconscious power work for you consistently and predictably all the days of your life.

▓ | ACTIVATE YOUR SUPERCONSCIOUS MIND

1 Think back over your life and recall a time when you had a superconscious experience that solved a problem or enabled you to achieve a goal. Reflect on the process and think about how you can duplicate it.

2 Select your most important goal, your major definite purpose, and visualize it clearly, over and over, with complete confidence that it will materialize at exactly the right time for you.

3 Begin the daily practice of solitude and meditation. During this time, just let your mind relax and float from subject to subject until exactly the right answer to the right question pops into your mind.

4 Make it a practice to take action on a superconscious idea as soon as it comes into your mind. Don't hesitate. Have complete faith that only the best can happen when you trust in this power.

5 Try to solve your problem with single-minded concentration, and if that doesn't work, get your mind busy elsewhere. At exactly the right time, the ideal solution will emerge from your intuition or appear in your life.

Your superconscious mind works for you in direct proportion to your complete trust and confidence in it. Practice letting go on a regular basis and wait patiently until exactly the right answer comes to you at exactly the right time.

18

Remain Flexible at All Times

*When I have finally decided that a result is worth getting,
I go ahead on it and make trial after trial until it comes.*

—THOMAS EDISON

It is in the nature of things that some people will be more successful and happier than others. Some people will make more money, have better lives, enjoy greater fulfillment and satisfaction, have happier relationships, and contribute more to their communities. Others will not.

The Menninger Institute of Kansas City conducted a study not long ago to determine what qualities would be most important for success and happiness in the twenty-first century. They concluded, after extensive research, that the most important single quality that you can develop, in a time of rapid change, is flexibility.

The opposite of flexibility is rigidity, an unwillingness to change in the face of new information or circumstances. The opposite of flexible thinking is fixed or *mechanical thinking*. The opposite of approaching life with an open mind is to react automatically and predictably in every situation. The quality of flexibility is therefore essential if you want to be, do, and have more than the average person.

The Speed of Change

Today, perhaps the most important factor affecting your life is the speed of change. We are living in an age where change is taking place at a faster rate than ever before in human history. And if anything, the rate of change is increasing, year by year.

Change today is not only faster, but it is also *discontinuous,* not following a straight line but starting, stopping, and moving in unpredictable directions. Change is coming at us from all sides and in so many different ways that it is often impossible to anticipate what might happen next.

By its very nature, change is unpredictable, often forcing us to scrap our very best plans and ideas overnight as the result of a completely new and unexpected development coming from a new and unexpected direction. As a result, we have to remain flexible in our thinking and in our possible courses of action.

A Major Cause of Stress

Change causes enormous stress for people who are fixed or rigid in their beliefs about how things "should be." They fall in love with what they are doing, with their current methods and processes, and are unwilling to change, even in the face of overwhelming evidence. Don't let this happen to you.

The only real question you should be asking about what you are doing is, Does it work? Is it achieving the end results desired? Based on the current situation, is this the best course of action? The only measure of the rightness or wrongness of a particular decision or course of action is its effectiveness in accomplishing the result desired or achieving the goal you have set. Keep asking, Does it work?

Three Factors Driving Change

Three factors are driving change today, each of them multiplying by each other to increase the speed of change.

The first change factor is the explosion of information and knowledge in every area of our lives. One new discovery or piece of information in a competitive marketplace can change the dynamics of your business overnight. A popular product or service or a major industry can be rendered obsolete by a new product or service that achieves the same result faster, better, cheaper, or easier than something else.

A critical news event, such as September 11, a market shock, such as that caused by Wall Street revelations, a scandal in a political party or industry can transform the thinking, actions, sales, and situation of an entire business or industry overnight.

For example, in 1989, when the Soviet Union dissolved, the Iron Curtain came down and the Cold War ended. The defense industry across America was severely shaken. Hundreds of thousands of highly trained and skilled men and women were laid off permanently. Entire industries were shut down and certain parts of the country were thrown into recession. The effects of change were overwhelming and unavoidable. Only the flexible were able to react and respond effectively.

Be Open to New Information

To remain flexible, you must be constantly open, alert to new ideas, information, and knowledge that can help you or hurt you in your business or in the achievement of your goals. One new idea can be enough to make or lose you a fortune. One idea can start you on the road to riches or knock you off it. One piece of information, at the right time, can save you enormous amounts of time, trouble, and money. Lack of that information can cost you a fortune.

All leaders are *readers*. It is absolutely essential that you keep current in your field. Read the magazines and publications published by your industry. Read the best-selling books in your field. Attend seminars and conferences. Join your industry associations and network with other people in your business. The power is always on the side of the person with the best and most current information.

The Tide of New Technology

The second factor driving change is the rapid growth and development of new technology. Every new piece of scientific or technical knowledge leads to an advance in technology aimed at helping people and companies get things done faster, better, cheaper, or easier. And the speed of technological change is increasing every day.

The rule is, Whatever works is already obsolete. A new piece of high-tech equipment put on the shelf is obsolete before it is unpacked. New technology today has a shelf life of six months before it is replaced by something that will do the job faster and cheaper. If you are not looking for ways to replace your product or service with something better, you can be assured that your competitors are staying up late at night looking for ways to put you out of business.

Playing Leapfrog

Being in business today is like playing an endless game of leapfrog. You look for a way to leapfrog over your competitor and serve your customers better, faster, and cheaper. Your competitor then leapfrogs over you with a newer or better product or service. You quickly regroup and leap over your competitor with a new innovation or improvement. Your competitor then leaps over you, and the game goes on without end.

The same principle of accelerating obsolescence applies to your products, your services, your processes, and especially to your sales and marketing strategies. It applies to your current advertising and methods of promotion. Whatever works will soon stop working. Either customers will become bored with it, your competitors will copy it, or it will no longer attract customers in the current marketplace.

Expect to Be Imitated

Not long ago, I hired an advertising agency and paid them $10,000 to develop an ad for me, which I then ran in a national newspaper. It was a powerful ad and drew a lot of good responses. We were walking around the office patting each other on the back until the following week, when a competitor used the identical ad that we had paid to have created but aimed at selling his product rather than ours. Our response rate dropped by 50 percent and continued to fall. And there was very little that we could do.

You must be continually developing backup plans for every aspect of your business, knowing without doubt that whatever you are doing it will soon stop working and will have to be replaced by something else that does.

Watch Out for the Comfort Zone

Earlier I discussed the "comfort zone" and how both individuals and organizations often fall into it and keep on doing the same things, over and over, whether they are working or not.

Sometimes the greatest danger to your long-term success can be short-term success. Success in any area can quickly breed complacency and a reluctance to change in response to the new realities of the marketplace. Don't let this happen to you.

Competitive Pressures Are Unending

The third element driving change and requiring greater flexibility is *competition*. Your competitors—local, national, and international—are more determined and creative today than they have ever been before. They are constantly looking for ways to take your customers away, steal your sales, reduce your cash flow, and if possible, put you out of business. They are aggressively selling their products or services using every argument and advantage they can possibly develop to undermine your position in the marketplace. Your competitors are aggressively using new information and technology to render you obsolete and to gain a competitive advantage.

Today, there are more companies, products, services, and salespeople than there are customers or buyers for them. The competition is becoming tougher and more intense. If you want to survive and thrive in this market, you must become even more focused and determined yourself. Above all, you must be flexible.

Zero-Base Everything Regularly

Earlier, I discussed the importance of "zero-based thinking" in examining every part of your life and activities today. Zero-based thinking is a vital tool in remaining flexible as well.

Continually ask, Is there anything that I am doing today that knowing what I now know I wouldn't start again if I had to do it over?

Look at every part of your life and business. Wherever you experience stress, resistance, or lack of success, ask the zero-based thinking question. And if there is something that you would not start again today, make plans immediately to stop and to channel your resources and energies where you can get better results.

Don't let your ego cloud your judgment or your common sense. Be more concerned with *what's right* rather than *who's right*. You must be open to the fact that most of your decisions will turn out to be *wrong* eventually. Be prepared to be flexible, especially in the face of new information, technology, or competition.

Three Magic Statements

There are three statements that you can learn to say, over and over, to remain flexible in turbulent times. Here they are:

The first is, *"I was wrong."* Most people would rather bluff, bluster, and deny rather than admit that they were wrong. What makes the refusal to admit you are wrong even worse is when everyone around you already knows that you are wrong. You are the only one who is fooling anyone, and that one person you are attempting to fool is yourself. When you realize that you are wrong, the smartest thing you can do is to admit it quickly, solve the problem, and get on with achieving the goal or result.

It has been estimated that as much as 80 percent of the time and energy of the key people in large companies and organizations is devoted to covering up the fact that they are wrong, and they don't want to admit it. Many companies, small and large, have gone bankrupt because of a refusal or failure to admit an obvious mistake.

Admit That You Are Not Perfect

The second statement that you must learn to say to remain flexible is, "I made a mistake." It is amazing how much time, energy, and money is wasted because some people's egos are so large that they will not admit they have made a mistake, even one that is obvious to everyone around them.

Once you say, "I was wrong" or "I made a mistake," the issue is largely over. From then on, everybody can get on with resolving the problem or achieving the goal. But as long as a key person is unwilling to admit that he or she has taken the wrong course, everything comes to a stop.

We have seen this repeatedly in national politics where the failure of a single person to admit a mistake or blunder has led to tremendous waste of time and energy for everyone involved and often for the entire nation.

Adapt to New Information Quickly

The third statement you should learn to say quickly and easily is "I changed my mind." If you get new information that contradicts the information upon which you made a previous decision, be prepared to admit candidly that you changed your mind.

It is not a weakness or a character flaw to be wrong, to make a mistake, or to change your mind. In fact, in a time of rapid change in the areas of knowledge, technology, and competition, it is a mark of courage, character, and flexibility to be willing to "cut your losses" quickly and practice the "reality principle" in everything you do.

Be willing to deal with the world as it is, rather than the way you wish it were or the way that it might have been in the past. Face the truth, whatever it is. Be honest with your-self and everyone around you.

Remain Open to New Realities

Always be open to reevaluating your goals and objectives in the light of new information, technology, or competition. Based on what you now know, is this the best course of action? If it is not, what else should you do? What else could you do?

If it is a goal, and the circumstances under which you made the goal have changed dramatically, be sure that you still want it badly enough to struggle and sacrifice for it. Be willing to drop it and set a new goal if you have changed your mind or if the goal is no longer as important to you today as it once was.

In a time of rapid change, resolve to be the first to recognize and embrace change when it occurs. Expect it as part of the normal and natural course of events. Refuse to be surprised or upset when events do not work out the way you thought they would or should.

Be Flexible in Your Relationships

Especially, be flexible with the important people in your life—your family, your friends, your coworkers, and your customers. Be open to differing points of view and different ideas. Be continually willing to admit that you could be wrong because you often are.

One of the characteristics of the best leaders is that they are good *listeners*. They ask a lot of questions and take in all the information possible before making up their minds or coming to a final conclusion. They also admit failure and cut their losses quickly when they make a mistake so they can move on to bigger and better things.

The Theory of Precession

There is another aspect of flexibility that you should bear in mind for the rest of your life and career. Buckminster Fuller, the scientist and philosopher, called it the "Theory of Precession," words that do not appear in any dictionary or encyclopedia. Dr. Robert Ronstadt of Babson College called the concept the "Corridor Principle." Napoleon Hill referred to this finding by the most successful people in America by saying that "within every setback or obstacle there lies the seed of an equal or greater opportunity or benefit."

What this theory means is that when you set a new goal for yourself, you will have a general idea of the steps you should take and the direction you should pursue. But almost inevitably, you will run into unexpected roadblocks that make it impossible to continue in that direction. However, by some miracle, just as you reach a wall, another door of opportunity will open along the corridor to success.

Because you are flexible, you will quickly take advantage of the new opportunity and begin moving in that direction, developing that new product or service, selling into that new market or customer base. But as you move down this new corridor, you will run into another obstacle or roadblock that might again block your progress. Just as you hit this new wall or obstruction, however, another opportunity will open up for you and take you down a different corridor toward your goal.

This may happen several times, with several false starts. In almost every case, you will achieve your greatest success in an area very different from what you initially planned. The key is to remain flexible.

Be Both Clear and Flexible

Here is the most important rule of flexibility: **"Be clear about your goal but be flexible about the process of achieving it."**

Always be open to the influence of your superconscious mind. Remain sensitive to the possibility of serendipitous and synchronous events. Be open to ideas, inspirations, and inputs from other people. In Matthew 18:13, Jesus says, "You must become like a little child if you would enter into the Kingdom of Heaven."

One interpretation of these words is that you must remain open-minded, flexible, calm, confident, and curious if you want to be able to recognize new opportunities and possibilities as they open up around you on your journey toward your goal.

Resolve to remain flexible and open, no matter what happens. Remember, there is almost always a *better* way to accomplish any task or to achieve any goal. Your aim should be to be alert and aware of what it might be, to find it, and then to take action in that new direction as quickly as possible. This will insure that you inevitably reach your goal, sometimes in the most unexpected and surprising ways.

▓ | REMAIN FLEXIBLE AT ALL TIMES

1 Regularly ask yourself the question, What do I really, really want to do with my life? and then make sure that your current goals and activities are in harmony with your answer.

2 Be completely honest and realistic with your life and goals. Resolve to see the world as it is, not as you wish it were or as it could be. What changes does this practice suggest?

3 Be willing to admit, in each area of your life where you experience stress or resistance, that you could be wrong or that you have made a mistake. Resolve today to cut your losses wherever possible.

4 If the situation has changed, or you have new information, be willing to change your mind and make a new decision based on the facts as they exist today. Refuse to persist in a course of action that does not make good sense.

Look into each problem or obstacle you face and seek the valuable lesson or benefit it contains. Should you change your direction or course of action based on new information or experience? If so, do it now.

19

Unlock Your
Inborn Creativity

Make every thought, every fact, that comes into your
mind pay you a profit. Make it work and produce for
you. Think of things not as they are but as they may be.
Don't merely dream but create!

—ROBERT COLLIER

Tony Buzan is a brain expert. He is the past president of
Mensa, an organization open only to people who score in the
top 2 percent on standardized IQ tests, and the author of several books on creativity, learning, and intelligence. According
to him, and to many other authorities in the field, the mental
potential of the average person is largely untapped and virtually unlimited.

Your neocortex, your thinking brain, has approximately
one hundred billion cells or neurons. Each of these cells bris-
tles like a porcupine with as many as twenty thousand gan-
glia or fibers that connect it to other brain cells. These cells
are, in turn, connected and interconnected to thousands and
millions of other cells, like an electric grid that lights up and
powers a large city. Each cell, and each connection contains
an element of mental energy or information that is available
to every other cell. This means that the complexity of your
brain is therefore beyond belief or imagination.

According to Tony Buzan and other brain experts, the
number of combinations and permutations of brain connections you have is greater than the number of molecules in the

known universe. It would be the equivalent of the number one followed by eight pages of zeros, row after row and page after page.

Enormous Reserve Capacity

As mentioned earlier, on average people use about 1 percent or 2 percent of their brain capacity for 100 percent of their functioning in life and work. The rest is "reserve capacity" that is seldom tapped or used for any reason. Most people "go to their graves with their music still in them."

You do not need to achieve a miracle to bring about spectacular results in your life. You only need to use a little bit more of your existing brainpower than you are using today. This small improvement in your thinking ability can change your life so profoundly that both you and others will be astonished by what you accomplish in the months and years ahead.

According to research conducted by Professor Sergei Yeframov in Russia some years ago, if you could use just 50 percent of your existing mental capacity, you could complete the doctoral requirements of a dozen universities, learn a dozen languages with ease and memorize the entire twenty-two volumes of the *Encyclopedia Britannica*.

Double Your Income?

If you are currently using only 2 percent of your mental potential and you could increase that to 4 percent, you could double your income, shoot ahead in your profession, rise to the top of your field, and transform your life. If you could use 5 percent or 6 percent or 7 percent of your potential, you would begin performing at a level that would amaze yourself and everyone around you. It was estimated that even Albert Einstein never used more than 10 percent to 15 percent of his mental potential at the height of his powers, and he was considered to be one of the greatest geniuses who ever lived.

Creativity Is a Natural Ability

Fully 95 percent of children tested between the ages of three and five are rated as highly creative. Of the same children tested again as teenagers, only about 5 percent are rated highly creative. What happened to them in the interim? As they went through school, they were taught that if you want to get along, you go along. They learned not to challenge the teacher or to suggest unusual ideas. In their attempts to be liked and accepted by their peers, they allowed their creativity to die down, like a fire without fuel.

The good news is that creativity is a natural and normal ability, possessed in quantity by virtually everyone. It is inborn, a part of your genetic structure, a faculty that is uniquely human. Everyone is creative. Fully 95 percent of the population has the ability to function at exceptional, if not *genius* levels, given the right situation and circumstances.

Use It or Lose It

But your creativity is like a muscle. If you don't use it, you lose it. Just like a muscle, if you do not exercise your creativity and stretch it regularly, it becomes weak and ineffective. Your ability to generate ideas must be constantly utilized to be kept in top condition.

Fortunately, at any time, you can begin tapping into your creativity and using it at a higher level. You can actually begin activating more neurons and dendrites in your brain, creating more and more connections and interconnections. Each time you use more of your existing brainpower, you become even more capable of thinking better and with greater clarity.

Ideas Are the New Source of Wealth

Today, we are in the information age. For the rest of your life, ideas will be the major source of new wealth. Ideas contain the keys to solving every problem. They are the most important tools for achieving any goals. And since your ability to generate new ideas is largely unlimited, your ability to achieve any goal you set for yourself is unlimited as well.

All wealth comes from *adding value,* from producing more, better, cheaper, faster, and easier than someone else. One good idea for adding value is all you need to start a fortune.

When you have clear goals—written and rewritten, visualized and emotionalized—you trigger your conscious, subconscious, and superconscious minds into generating a continuous flow of ideas for goal attainment.

Solve Any Problem

There is no problem you cannot solve, no obstacle you cannot overcome, and no goal that you cannot achieve by tapping into your creative mind exactly as it is today. You have far more intelligence and mental potential right now than you could ever use, even if you lived one hundred years. Just because you have not accessed all of your mental powers up until now does not mean that you cannot begin using them from this day forward.

Physical fitness and mental fitness are very similar in some respects. If you want to become physically fit, you have to work out and engage in physical exercise. If you want to build physical muscles, you must "pump iron" and drive new blood into your muscles by straining them with dumbbells or barbells. The more stress you put on your muscles, the stronger they become over time.

Your mind is very similar. In order to build your mental muscles, you have to "pump *mental* iron." You have to put stress and strain on your brain, concentrating all of your mental energies to generate ideas and solutions and to solve problems on the way to your goals.

Practice Mindstorming Regularly

The most powerful technique for improving your intelligence and increasing your creativity is what I call "mindstorming." The way it works is simple. The results that you get will be so amazing as to be life changing.

You begin the mindstorming process by first getting a clean sheet of paper. At the top of this page you write your goal or problem in the form of a question. The simpler and more specific the question, the better will be the quality of the answers that you generate in response to it.

For example, instead of writing a question like, "How can I make more money?" you would write, "How can I double my income in the next twenty-four months?"

Even better, if you are earning $50,000 per year today, your question should be, "How can I earn $100,000 per year by December 31 (of a specific year)?"

Each of your answers should be written using the "Three *P* Formula." It should be personal, positive, and in the present tense. In other words, your answers should be written as affirmations or instructions from your conscious mind to your subconscious mind. Often, you will write down answers on this sheet and promptly forget them. Then, sometime later, as a result of superconscious functioning, you will attract into your life an opportunity to put one of your answers into action.

Mastering the Method

Once you have written your question at the top of the page, you then discipline yourself to generate at least twenty answers to that question. You can write down more than twenty answers to the question, but it is essential in this exercise that you set a goal for a minimum of twenty.

Your first three to five answers will be easy. You will quickly come up with answers like "work harder," "start earlier and stay later," "work on higher value tasks."

Your next five answers will be more difficult. You will have to think hard and dig deeper to come up with less obvious but more creative ways to answer your question.

Your last ten answers will be the most difficult of all. Many people find this part of the exercise so difficult that their minds go blank. Their eyes glaze over. They become light-headed with the rush of blood to their brains that takes place when they begin this process of "pumping mental iron."

However, no matter how long it takes, especially the first few times you practice this exercise, you must discipline yourself to keep writing until you have at least twenty answers. Sometimes the twentieth answer that you generate will be the breakthrough answer that enables you to save yourself thousands of dollars and many hours of hard work.

Often, your last answer is the inspired idea that changes your life and career.

Select One Action

Once you have at least twenty answers, go back over your list and review your answers. Then select at least one action that you can take immediately to begin moving yourself more rapidly toward your goal or toward solving the problem.

You can multiply the effectiveness of this process by taking the very best answer that you identified in the first list of twenty and writing it at the top of a fresh sheet of paper in the form of a question. Then see if you cannot generate twenty answers to that question as well. This combination exercise will rev you up mentally, like stepping on the accelerator of a car while the transmission is in neutral. Your mind will sparkle and dance with mental energy and bristle with ideas like the bright lights of a Christmas tree.

For example, your first question could be, "How can I double my income to $100,000 over the next twenty-four months?" One of your answers could be, "I work two extra hours each day."

You could transfer this answer to a new sheet of paper and phrase it as a question: "What can I do to get two extra hours of productive time each day?" You can then begin writing twenty different things that you can do to save time, gain time, and spend two additional hours on productive work each day.

Whatever answer you choose, put it into action *immediately*. Do something. Do anything. The faster you take action on this exercise, the greater and more continuous will be the flow of ideas as you go through the day. If you generate these ideas and then do nothing with them, the creative flow will slow down and stop.

Use Mindstorming on Every Goal

The very best time to do this exercise is first thing in the morning, right after you have rewritten your goals in your spiral notebook. Each morning, you can take one goal, re-write it as a question, and then generate twenty answers to that question. You can then immediately get busy and implement one of your answers.

You can perform this exercise repeatedly on the same goal if the goal is big enough and important enough to you. Don't worry about writing down the same answers over and over again. The more you practice this exercise, the more likely it is that you will trigger completely unexpected breakthrough ideas. This may require several days or even weeks of work before the flash of inspiration takes place. You must be patient and determined. It will come.

The Cumulative Power of Idea Generation

Imagine that you were to perform this exercise every morning five days per week. You can take the weekends off to relax your brain. If you did this exercise five days per week, you would generate one hundred ideas per week. If you practiced this exercise fifty weeks per year, you would generate five thousand ideas over the course of the next twelve months. And you don't even have to think on your vacation!

If you were then to implement one new idea each day to help you to move faster toward your goals, that would work out to one idea per day, multiplied by five days per week, multiplied by fifty weeks per year. This would amount to 250 new ideas per year that you would implement in your life.

Now here is a question: Do you think that this exercise, conducted regularly, would have an impact on your life and future? In a world where most people have very few ideas at all during the year, do you think that this exercise would give you an edge in your field? Do you think that if you did this every day, you would soon become wealthy and successful in anything to which you applied yourself? I think the answer is clear.

One good idea can save you years of hard work or thousands of dollars. A multiple of good ideas, one after the other, building on each other, will make you rich, happy, and successful, virtually without fail.

Focus on the Solution

As mentioned earlier, successful people are intensely *solution oriented*. The fact is that life is a continuous succession of problems and difficulties without end. This river of problems is only interrupted by the occasional *crisis,* which makes the problems seem small in comparison.

In fact, if you are living a busy life, you will probably experience a crisis of some kind every two to three months throughout your life. You will have business crises, family crises, financial crises, health crises, and other crises. The problems and crises never stop. They keep coming, like the waves of the ocean. The only aspect you can control is your *responses* to these problems and crises. And therein lies the key to your success.

Successful people respond effectively to problems. Ineffective people do not. Successful people take a deep breath, relax, and think clearly. They look for the good in every situation. They seek the valuable lesson. Above all, they focus on the solution, on what can be done, rather than on what has happened and who is to blame.

Deal with Each Problem Effectively

Just as there is a process for solving mathematical problems, there is a process for solving business and life problems, and you can learn it and use it for the rest of your career. It requires that you approach the business of problem solving systematically and in an organized fashion.

- **Step one: Define the problem clearly.**
 A problem properly defined is half solved. It is absolutely amazing how much time is wasted floundering around looking for a solution when no one is quite clear about the problem.

- **Step two: Ask, What are all the possible causes of this problem?**
 Look for both the obvious and the not-so-obvious causes of the problem. How did it begin? What are its origins? What triggered it in the first place? What is the critical variable that changed to cause the problem? What assumptions were made that led to the problem? Just like a doctor conducting an intensive examination on a sick patient, you should thoroughly dissect the problem before you attempt to solve it.

- **Step three: Ask, What are all the possible solutions?**
 Avoid the natural tendency of most human beings to leap from a problem definition to a conclusion regarding a

solution of some kind. Always ask, "What is another solution?"

Sometimes the best solution is to do nothing at all. Sometimes the best solution is to gather more information. Sometimes the best solution is to realize that this is not your problem and pass it onto someone else whose responsibility it is.

- **Step four: Ask, What must this solution *accomplish*?**

Once you have identified several possible solutions, the only way you can judge the attractiveness of a solution is to determine, in advance, what you want the solution to accomplish.

You've heard it said that "The operation was a success, but the patient died." It is very common for us to initiate a solution and implement it, but the problem is not only not solved, but it is worse than it was before we took action.

Be sure that the solution you select will accomplish the purpose you had in mind when you started the problem-solving exercise.

- **Step five: Assign specific responsibility or take responsibility yourself for implementing the solution.**

Once you have decided on the ideal solution, set a deadline for implementation. Set a measure by which you can determine if the solution has been effective.

A problem-solving discussion that does not lead to agreement on a specific solution, accompanied by the assignment of personal responsibility and a deadline, is a problem that will come back again and again without resolution.

Practice this systematic method of dealing with a problem until it becomes a habit. You will be amazed at how much more effective you become and how much better your results will be using this method.

The Key to Victory and Success

In studying warfare and battles over the centuries, I have always been fascinated by the situations where a smaller force defeated a numerically superior force. In every case, what I discovered was that the numerically smaller force was far better organized, more methodical, and more orderly in its plan of attack and execution than was the larger, more disorganized force.

By the same token, an ordinary person, with a system or recipe for problem solving, can run circles around highly intelligent or well-educated people who throw themselves at their problems without a method or process for solving them.

These two methodologies, mindstorming and the systematic approach, give you a tremendous advantage in mastering the inevitable problems and difficulties of life.

Write It Down

Always be sure to *think* on paper. Write things down. There is something that happens between the brain and the hand when you write. You get a greater sense of clarity and understanding with regard to the issues involved. You think better. Your perception is sharper. You actually become smarter and more creative by the very act of writing everything down as you go along and before you make a decision.

Play Down the Chessboard

One of the most powerful creative thinking exercises you can practice is called "scenario planning." In scenario planning, think several moves forward in the game of life and imagine what might happen sometime in the future.

Even though the future is largely unknowable, certain trends taking place today will continue into the future. Certain events taking place around you will affect these trends, if not interrupt them in different ways. Completely unexpected events will arise that will require you to change your plans completely.

Answer Two Questions

In scenario planning, you ask yourself two questions. First, What are the three worst things that could possibly happen in the months or years ahead that would negatively affect my business or my personal life?

Write them down. Be brutally honest with yourself. Refuse to wish or hope for the best. For example, imagine that your best customer went out of business or was unable to pay you for the products or services that you had sold to him. What would you do? How would you react? What steps could you take to guard against this eventuality?

Next, ask yourself, What are the three best things that could possibly happen to me in the months and years ahead?

With your answers to both of these questions, you can use mindstorming to prepare yourself for any eventuality. If it is a potential setback, ask yourself, How could we guard against this setback? Then generate twenty answers to this question.

If it is a possible opportunity, ask yourself, How could we increase the likelihood of this opportunity taking place or take advantage of this opportunity as it is today? Write out twenty answers to this question as well.

Each time you ask yourself one of these questions, like an electric spark you will trigger ideas and insights. The more you think about these key questions, the more you will activate your superconscious mind to give you insights and flashes of inspiration that will enable you to seize opportunities or avoid dangers.

Develop Your Options

One of the most important parts of your personal philosophy should revolve around the development of options. The rule is, You are only as free as your well-developed alternatives.

If your goal is to be happy, successful, and free, you must have *choices*. There must be more than *one* step that you can take, in every situation. You can never allow yourself to be trapped with only one course of action open to you.

From the time you take your first job, make your first investment, or embark on any part of life, you should immediately begin to develop an alternative to that, if something should go wrong.

Develop Your Plan B

Otto von Bismarck, the "Iron Chancellor" of nineteenth century Germany, was considered to be the finest statesmen of his age. He was able to juggle competing nations, principalities, and powers against each other in the process of forming Germany into a unified state. His political life was an endless process of negotiating back and forth, winning and losing time after time.

Bismarck was famous for always having a backup plan completely developed before he began negotiations on his main plan. This became known as a "Bismarck Plan," a "Plan B." You should always have a Plan B for the important parts of your business and personal life as well.

What is your Plan B? What is your backup plan if your current job, career, industry, or course of action does not work out successfully? What is your backup plan if your current investments do not work out or if your "best-laid plans" fail? What are your alternatives? What would you do if you found yourself out on the street tomorrow or in the position of having to start over?

The more options you have, the greater mental freedom you have as well. The more alternatives you have thought through and developed, the greater power you will have in any situation. The more that you have developed different courses of action in case the one you are following does not work out, the greater confidence you will have. This is why one of the most important things you can do throughout life is to increase the range of your "freedom of action." Use your creativity to develop options and alternatives continually, no matter how well things are going at the moment.

Long-Term Thinking

Your ultimate goal in your business and your career is to earn as much money as possible and to achieve financial independence. All profit, all financial success in our society comes from "adding value" of some kind. When you add value, you put yourself into a position to capture some of that value in the form of increased income, profit, or dividends. This is the basic law of all market economics, and like most basic economic laws, it is unknown or misunderstood by most people working in our society today.

One of the questions you can ask in your mindstorming exercise is, What can I do to increase my value to my customers today?

You might ask, Who are my *ideal* customers? What can I do to attract more of my ideal customers into buying from me?

Best of all, you should ask, What would I have to do to deserve more of exactly the kind of customers that I want to have? What could you do more of, or start doing, to be more deserving of having more of the customers you really want?

Add Value Continually

Always be looking for ways to use your creativity to add value by doing things faster, better, cheaper, or easier in some way. Just as the word "deserve" comes from the Latin roots *de* and *servus,* which mean "from service," you should always be looking for ways to deserve greater rewards from serving your customers better in some way.

In the final analysis, as a member of society, as a "player" in our economic system, your riches and rewards will come from your ability to serve other people better than your competitors do. Use your intelligence and your creativity every single day to find ways to make yourself more valuable to your company, your industry, and your world. This is the true hallmark of personal genius.

⚏ | UNLOCK YOUR INBORN CREATIVITY

1 Select your most important goal or biggest problem, and write it at the top of a sheet of paper as a question. Then discipline yourself to generate twenty answers to that question, and implement one of those answers immediately.

2 Approach every problem systematically by defining it clearly, developing possible solutions, making a decision, and then implementing the solution as soon as possible.

3 Think on paper. Write down every detail of a problem or goal and look for simple, practical ways to solve the problem or achieve the goal.

4 Identify the best and worst events that could happen to you in the months ahead. Determine what you could do to reduce the effects of the worst outcomes and maximize the benefits or likelihood of the best possible outcomes.

You are only as free as your options. Develop a Plan B for every important area of your business and personal life.

20

Do Something Every Day

My success evolved from working hard
at the business at hand every day.

—JOHNNY CARSON

Many studies have been conducted over the years to try to determine why it is that some people are more successful than others. Hundreds, and even thousands of salespeople, staff, and managers have been interviewed, tested, and studied in an attempt to identify the common denominators of success. One of the most important success factors discovered, over and over again, is the quality of "action orientation."

Successful people are *intensely* action oriented. They seem to move faster than unsuccessful people. They are busier. They try more, and they try harder. They start a little earlier and they stay a little later. They are in constant motion.

Unsuccessful people, on the other hand, start at the last moment necessary and quit at the first moment possible. They are fastidious about taking every minute of coffee breaks, lunch hours, sick leave, and vacations. They sometimes brag, "When I am not at work, I never even think about it."

A Story of Failure

We used to have an employee who was always late. When we spoke to him about this, he explained that his reason for being late was the traffic. We suggested to him that he leave earlier so that the traffic would not be a problem. He was shocked. He said, "But if I left earlier and there was no traffic, I might arrive at work earlier than my starting time. I couldn't possibly do that!"

Needless to say, we soon let him go and hired someone else with a greater sense of responsibility and commitment. We heard later that he has continued on with the endless round of part-time jobs and unemployment that has marked his career. His attitude has set him up for failure time and time again.

The Law of Compensation

In his famous essay "Compensation," Ralph Waldo Emerson wrote that you will always be compensated in life in direct proportion to the value of your contribution. If you want to increase the size of your rewards, you must increase the quality and quantity of your results. If you want to get more out, you have to put more in. There is no other way.

Napoleon Hill found that the key quality of successful men and women, most of whom started at the bottom, many of them penniless, was that early in life, they developed the habit of "going the extra mile." They discovered, as the old saying goes, that "There are never any traffic jams on the extra mile."

The Quality of Self-Made Millionaires

In one study of self-made millionaires, researchers interviewed thousands of men and women who had started with nothing and who had accumulated more than a million dollars in the course of their careers. These self-made millionaires almost unanimously agreed that their success was the result of always doing more than they were paid for. They had made it a habit from their first jobs to always put in more than they took out. They were always looking for ways to contribute beyond what was expected of them.

Lifelong Career Success

When I speak to a graduating class of business students, they often ask me, usually with some concern, if I can give them some suggestions or ideas on what they can do to be successful in the world of work. I always give them the same advice. It worked for me when I was a young man and it works for everybody at every stage of his or her career.

My advice consists of two parts. First, as soon as you get settled in at your new job and you are on top of your work, go to your boss and tell him or her that you want "more responsibility." Say that you are determined to make the maximum contribution possible in this organization and that you would very much like more responsibility whenever it becomes available.

When I first started doing this as a young executive with a large corporation, my boss nodded and smiled and thanked me for my interest. But nothing happened, at least for a while. Every few days, I would report to my boss and mention, in parting, that I wanted more responsibility.

Your Chance Will Come

After a few weeks of this, my boss gave me a project to study and evaluate. I jumped on it like a dog jumping on a bone and ran off. I worked day and night and throughout the weekend, tearing that project apart, gathering research, reassembling the details, and putting together a report and a proposal. On Monday morning, I went back to my boss with a complete proposal on the project. He was obviously surprised. He said, "There was no rush. I didn't expect anything back from you for a week or two."

I thanked him for his concern and told him that "This project evaluation is complete, as you requested. And by the way, I would really like more responsibility."

Things began to change for me very soon after that project evaluation. A week later, I was given another small task, completely outside my range of duties. Again, I grabbed the task and completed it to the best of my ability. A week or two later, my boss gave me another task and then a week later, still another task.

In every case, whatever it was, whether I knew anything about it or not, I immediately went to work on it, often on my own time and on the weekends. I would get it done and back to my boss as fast as I could.

Move Fast on Opportunities

This brings me to my second piece of advice for anyone who wants to be successful in his or her career. Once you get the responsibility that you have asked for, complete it quickly and well and get it back to your boss as fast as you can, as though it were a grenade with the pin pulled out. Move quickly. Don't delay.

It is absolutely amazing the positive impression you will make on other people when you keep asking for more responsibility, and then when you get the responsibility, you complete the task quickly.

Very soon, my boss had marked me as the "go-to guy." Whenever something came up that he needed handled immediately, he called me rather than any of the other executives, some of whom had been working there for several years. In no time, I began to move up in the organization.

Be Prepared for Your Opportunity

One day, he threw me a task, like a football to a tight end in a close game, which I caught and ran with for a touchdown. By acting quickly, flying a thousand miles and working day and night, I discovered a fraud and saved the company 2 million dollars. If I had delayed even a couple of days, the money would have been lost forever.

After that success, the dam broke. First I was given a large assignment and then responsibility for an entire new division and then another new division and then a third. By the time I had been working for that company for two years, I was running three divisions involving almost 50 million dollars' worth of business activities and managing a staff of more than fifty people in three offices.

Meanwhile, my coworkers were still coming in at 9 o'clock sharp, going for lunch with each other, and quitting at 5 o'clock to go for drinks at the bar. They muttered and told each other that the reason I was moving up was because I was "lucky" or the boss was playing favorites. They never learned the importance of asking for more responsibility and moving fast.

A Secret of Success

The retiring president of the U.S. Chamber of Commerce, many years ago, told a story at his going away dinner. He had become one of the most respected businesspeople in America and overseas. He had developed the kind of reputation for high-quality work that every person in business dreams of having.

He said that when he was a young man, unsuccessful and frustrated, he came across a saying written on a brown lunch bag and posted on a high school bulletin board. As he passed the bulletin board, something caused him to stop, and he read the words on the lunch bag. They said, "Your success in life will be in direct proportion to what you do after you do what you are expected to do."

He told the audience that these words changed his life. Up to that time in his career, he felt that he was doing a good job because he was doing what he had been told to do, what he was expected to do. But from that point onward, he resolved that he would do far more than what was expected of him. He resolved that he would always go the extra mile and do more than he was paid for. From that day onward for the rest of his career, he got up a little earlier, worked a little harder, and stayed a little later. He moved faster from task to task and from customer to customer.

And here is what always happens. The faster he moved, the more experience he got. The more experience he got, the better he got at his job. The better he got, the better results he got in the same period of time. In no time at all, he was being paid more and promoted faster.

By moving faster and always doing more than expected, he had shifted onto the fast track in his career and began moving ahead rapidly. He was soon promoted into a new department then hired into a new industry and given a new area of responsibility. In each case, he had one strategy. Do more than you are paid for. Do more than others expect. Go the extra mile. Get busy. Get going. Take action. Don't waste time. And he never looked back.

Wisdom of a Founding Father

Thomas Jefferson wrote, "Determine never to be idle. No person will have occasion to complain of the want of time, who never loses any. It is wonderful how much may be done, if we are always doing."

Later, he wrote, "The rising sun has never caught me in bed in my entire life."

The Time Will Pass Anyway

Here's an important point. The time is going to pass *anyway*. The weeks, months, and years of your life are going to go by in any case. The only question is, What are you going to do with this time?

Since the day is going to go past in any case, why not start a little earlier, work a little harder, and stay a little later? Why not put yourself on the side of the angels? Why not develop a reputation as the "go-to guy" (or gal) who everyone looks to when they need to get something done quickly and well? This will do more to put your foot on the accelerator of your career than anything else you can imagine.

Get Going and Keep Going

A key to high income is the "momentum principle of success." This principle says that it takes considerable energy to get yourself into motion and moving. But it takes much less energy to keep yourself moving, once you get going.

This momentum principle explains success as much as any other factor. Successful people are busy people. They get up and they get going and they keep going all day long. They work all the time they work. They are constantly in motion, like moving targets.

Plan Your Time Carefully

Successful people plan their days and hours and even their quarter-hours very carefully. In every study of this issue, there seems to be a direct relationship between tight time planning and high income. The highest paid professionals in our society, from whom come fully 25 percent of self-made millionaires in America, are lawyers, doctors, and other medical professionals. They all manage their time in terms of *minutes* spent on each case or with each patient.

The people who earn the very least in our society are those who think of their time in terms of the day, the week, or the month. They have no problem wasting the first half of the day. They justify this by saying they will catch up in the afternoon. Sometimes they waste the first couple of days of the week. They think that they will catch up later in the week. Sometimes they waste the first one or two weeks of the month.

The Fatal Flaw in Monthly Quotas

I have worked with countless sales organizations over the years. Fully 80 percent of the salespeople in these organizations, all of whom work on monthly quotas, take it easy for the first three weeks of the month and then suddenly go into a state of frantic activity during the last week, working desperately to make enough sales to hit their quotas.

But not the top people. The top people work on the first day of the month with the same focus and intensity that they worked on the last day of the previous month. They hit the road running, like a roadrunner. They put the "pedal to the metal" at seven or seven-thirty in the morning. They beat the morning rush hour traffic by getting in before anyone else, and they beat the evening rush hour traffic by staying and working long after everyone else has rushed out to sit on the freeway.

Generate Continuous Energy

Mentally and physically, the faster you move, the more energy you have. The faster you move, the happier you are and the more enthusiastic and creative you become. The faster you move, the more you get done, the more you get paid, and the more successful you feel.

Apply the momentum principle to your life. Once you start going, keep going. Alan Lakein, the time management specialist said, "Fast tempo is essential to success." Tom Peters said that all successful people have a "bias for action." The key to getting more done is for you to select your most important task and then to start it with a "sense of urgency." This is the real key to success and high achievement.

DO SOMETHING EVERY DAY

1 Resolve today to pick up the pace in your life. Move faster from task to task. Walk quickly. Develop a higher tempo of activity.

2 Imagine you were going away tomorrow for a month and you had to get caught up on everything before you left. Work as hard and as fast as you do just before you leave for vacation.

3 Practice tight time planning. Imagine that you only had half the time available to get the job done and work with a sense of urgency all day long.

4 Continually ask for more responsibility and when you get it, complete the task quickly and well. This one habit will continually open doors of opportunity for you.

From now on, resolve to get up one hour earlier and get going immediately. Work through lunchtime and coffee breaks. Stay an hour later to get caught up and ready for the next day. These additions will double your productivity and put you onto the fast track in your career.

21

Persist until You Succeed

Few things are impossible to diligence and skill;
great works are performed not by strength, but
by perseverance.

—SAMUEL JOHNSON

Every great success in your life will represent a triumph
of persistence. Your ability to decide what you want, to
begin, and then to persist through all obstacles and difficulties until you achieve your goals is the critical determinant of
your success. And the flip side of persistence is courage.

Perhaps the greatest challenge that you will ever face in
life is the conquest of fear and the development of the *habit*
of courage. Winston Churchill once wrote, "Courage is
rightly considered the foremost of the virtues, for upon it, all
others depend."

The Conquest of Fear

Fear is, and always has been, the greatest enemy of mankind.
When Franklin D. Roosevelt said, "The only thing we have
to fear is fear itself," he was saying that the *emotion* of fear,
rather than the reality of what we fear, is what causes us anxiety, stress, and unhappiness.

When you develop the habit of courage and unshakable
self-confidence, a whole new world of possibilities opens up

for you. Just think—what would you dare to dream or be or do if you weren't afraid of anything in the whole world?

You Can Learn Anything You Need to Learn

Fortunately, the habit of courage can be *learned* just as any other success skill is learned. To do so, you need to work to conquer your fears while simultaneously building up the kind of courage and confidence that will enable you to deal unafraid with the inevitable ups and downs of life.

Syndicated columnist Ann Landers wrote, "If I were asked to give what I consider the single most useful bit of advice for all humanity, it would be this: *Expect* trouble as an inevitable part of life, and when it comes, hold your head high. Look it squarely in the eye, and say, 'I will be bigger than you. You cannot defeat me.'" *This* is the kind of attitude that leads to victory.

The Causes and Cures of Fear

The starting point in overcoming fear and developing courage is, first of all, to look at the factors that predispose us toward being afraid.

As we know, the root source of fear is childhood conditioning, usually destructive criticism from one or both parents. This causes us to experience two types of fear. These are, first of all, the fear of failure, which causes us to think, I can't, I can't, I can't; and second, the fear of rejection, which causes us to think, I have to, I have to, I have to.

Because of these fears, we become preoccupied with the fear of losing our money or our time or our emotional investment in a relationship. We become hypersensitive to the opinions and possible criticisms of others, sometimes to the point where we are afraid to do anything that anyone else might disapprove of. Our fears tend to paralyze us, holding us back from taking constructive action in the direction of our dreams and goals. We hesitate. We become indecisive. We procrastinate. We make excuses and find reasons to delay. And finally, we feel frustrated, caught in the double bind of "I have to, but I can't," or "I can't, but I have to."

Fear and Ignorance Go Together

Fear can be caused by ignorance. When we have limited information, we may be tense and insecure about the outcome of our actions. Ignorance causes us to fear change, to fear the unknown, and to avoid trying anything new or different.

But the reverse is also true. The very act of gathering more information and experience in a particular area gives us more courage and confidence in that area. There are parts of your life where you have no fear at all because you have mastered that area, like driving a car, skiing, or selling and managing. Because of your knowledge and experience, you feel completely capable of handling whatever happens. You have no fears.

Fatigue Doth Make Cowards of Us All

Another factor that causes fear is illness or fatigue. When we are tired or unwell or when we are not physically fit, we are more predisposed to fear and doubt than when we are feeling healthy and happy and energetic.

Sometimes you can totally change your attitude toward yourself and your potential by getting a good night's sleep or taking a vacation long enough to completely recharge your mental and emotional batteries. Rest and relaxation build courage and confidence as much as any other factors.

Everyone Is Afraid

Here is an important point: All intelligent people are afraid of *something*. It is normal and natural to be concerned about your physical, emotional, and financial survival. The courageous person is not a person who is unafraid. As Mark Twain said, "Courage is resistance to fear, mastery of fear— not absence of fear."

It is not whether or not you are afraid. We are all afraid. The question is, How do you deal with the fear? The courageous person is simply one who goes forward in spite of the fear. And here is something else I have learned: when you *confront* your fears and move toward what you are afraid of, your fears diminish while at the same time your self-esteem and self-confidence increases.

However, when you *avoid* what you fear, your fears grow until they begin to control every aspect of your life. And as your fears increase, your self-esteem, your self-confidence, and your self-respect diminish accordingly. As the actor Glenn Ford once said, "If you do not do the thing you fear, the fear controls your life."

Analyze Your Fears

Once you have recognized the factors that can cause fear, the next step in overcoming fear is to sit down and take the time to objectively identify, define, and analyze your own personal fears.

At the top of a clean sheet of paper, write the question, "What am I afraid of?"

Begin filling out your list of fears by writing down everything, major and minor, over which you experience any anxiety. Start with the most common fears: the fears of failure or loss and the fears of rejection or criticism.

Some people, dominated by the fear of failure, invest an enormous amount of energy justifying or covering up their mistakes. They cannot deal with the idea of making a mistake. Others, preoccupied by the fear of rejection, are so sensitive to how they appear to others that they seem to have no ability to take independent action at all. Until they are absolutely certain that someone else will approve, they refrain from doing anything.

Set Priorities on Your Fears

Once you have made a list of every fear that you believe may be affecting your thinking and your behavior, organize the items in order of importance. Which fear do you feel has the greatest impact on your thinking or holds you back more than any other? Which fear would be number two? What would be your third fear? And so on.

With regard to your predominant fear, write the answers to these three questions:

1. How does this fear hold me back in life?
2. How does this fear help me, or how has it helped me in the past?
3. What would be my payoff for eliminating this fear?

Some years ago, I went through this exercise and concluded that my biggest fear was the fear of poverty. I was afraid of not having enough money, being broke, perhaps even being destitute. I knew that this fear had originated during my childhood because my parents, who grew up during the Depression, had continually worried about money. My fear was reinforced when I was broke at various times during my twenties. I could objectively assess the origins of this fear, but it still had a strong hold on me. Even when I had sufficient money for all my needs, this fear was always there.

My answer to the first question, "How does this fear hold me back?" was that it caused me to be anxious about taking risks with money. It caused me to play it safe with regard to employment. And it caused me to choose security over opportunity.

My answer to the second question, "How does this fear help me?" was that, in order to escape the fear of poverty, I had developed the habit of working much longer and harder than the average person. I was more ambitious and determined. I took much more time to study and learn about the various ways that money could be made and invested. The fear of poverty was, in effect, driving me toward financial independence.

When I answered the third question, "What would be my payoff for overcoming this fear?" I immediately saw that I would be willing to take more risks, I would be more aggressive in pursuing my financial goals, I could and would start my own business, and I would not be so tense and concerned about spending too much or having too little. Especially, I would no longer be so concerned about the price of everything.

By objectively analyzing my biggest fear in this way, I was able to begin the process of eliminating it. And so can you.

Practice Makes Permanent

You can begin the process of developing courage and eliminating fear by engaging in actions consistent with the behaviors of courage and self-confidence. Anything that you practice over and over eventually becomes a new habit. You develop courage by behaving courageously whenever courage is called for.

Here are some of the activities you can practice to develop the habit of courage. The first and perhaps most important kind of courage is the courage to *begin,* to launch, to step out in faith. This is the courage to try something new or different, to move out of your comfort zone with no guarantee of success.

Earlier I mentioned Dr. Robert Ronstadt of Babson College who taught entrepreneurship for many years. He conducted a study of those who took his class and found that only 10 percent actually started their own businesses and became successful later in life. He could find only one quality that the successful graduates had in common. It was their willingness to actually start their own businesses, as opposed to continually talking about it.

The Courage to Begin

He discovered the "Corridor Principle," that we mentioned earlier. As these individuals moved forward toward their goals, as though proceeding down a corridor, doors opened to them that they would not have seen if they had not been in forward motion.

It turned out that the graduates of his entrepreneurship course who had done nothing with what they had learned were still waiting for things to be *just right* before they began. They were unwilling to launch themselves down the corridor of uncertainty until they could somehow be assured that they would be successful—something that never happened.

The Future Belongs to the Risk Takers

The future belongs to the *risk takers,* not the security seekers. Life is perverse in the sense that the more you seek security, the less of it you have. But the more you seek opportunity, the more likely it is that you will achieve the security that you desire.

Whenever you feel fear or anxiety and you need to bolster your courage to persist in the face of obstacles and setbacks, switch your attention to your goals. Create a clear mental picture of the person that you would like to be, performing the way you would like to perform. Nothing is wrong with thoughts of fear as long as you temper them with thoughts of courage and self-reliance. Whatever you dwell upon, grows—so be careful.

The mastery of fear and the development of courage are essential prerequisites for a happy, successful life. With a commitment to acquire the habit of courage, you will eventually reach the point where your fears no longer play a major role in your decision making. You will set big, challenging, exciting goals, and you will be confident that you can attain them. You will be able to face every situation with calmness and self-assurance. The key is courage.

Learn from the Masters

What if you could sit down with one of the most successful men or women in our society and learn all the lessons of success that he or she had taken a lifetime to gather? Do you think that would help you to be more successful?

What if you could sit down with one hundred of the most successful men and women who ever lived and learn their rules, their lessons, and their secrets of success? Would that help you to be more successful in your own life? What if you could sit down, over time, with more than 1,000 highly successful men and women? How about 2,000 or 3,000?

Action Is Everything

Your answer is probably that spending time with these extremely successful men and women, learning what they learned in order to achieve their goals, would be of great help to you. The truth is, however, is that all of this advice and input would do you no good at all unless you took some specific action on what you had learned.

If learning about success was all that it took to do great things with your life, then your success would be guaranteed. The bookstores are full of self-help books, each one of them loaded with ideas that you can use to be more successful. The fact is, however, that all of the best advice in the world will only help you if you can motivate yourself to take persistent, continuous action in the direction of your goals until you succeed.

The probable result of your reading the ideas in this book has been that you have made some specific decisions about what you are going to do more of, and what you are going to do *less of.* You have set certain goals for yourself in different areas of your life, and you have made resolutions that you are determined to follow through on. The most important question for your future now is simply, Will you do what you have resolved to do?

Self-Discipline Is the Core Quality

The single most important quality for success is self-discipline. Self-discipline means that you have the ability, within yourself, based on your strength of character and willpower, to do what you should do, when you should do it, whether you feel like it or not.

Character is the ability to follow through on a resolution after the enthusiasm with which the resolution was made has passed. It is not what you learn that is decisive for your future. It is whether or not you can discipline yourself to pay the price, over and over, until you finally obtain your objective.

You need self-discipline in order to set your goals and to make plans for their accomplishment. You need self-discipline to continually revise and upgrade your plans with new information. You need self-discipline to use your time well and to always concentrate on the one most important task that you need to do at the moment. You need self-discipline to invest in yourself every day, to build yourself up personally and professionally, to learn what you need to learn in order to enjoy the success of which you are capable.

You need self-discipline to delay gratification, to save your money, and to organize your finances so that you can achieve financial independence in the course of your working lifetime. You need self-discipline to keep your thoughts on your goals and dreams and keep them off of your doubts and fears. You need self-discipline to respond positively and constructively in the face of every difficulty.

Persistence Is Self-Discipline in Action

Perhaps the most important demonstration of self-discipline is your level of persistence when the going gets tough. Persistence is self-discipline in action. Persistence is the true measure of individual human character. Your persistence is, in fact, the real measure of your belief in yourself and your ability to succeed.

Each time that you persist in the face of adversity and disappointment, you build up the habit of persistence. You build pride, power, and self-esteem into your character and your personality. You become stronger and more resolute. You deepen your levels of self-discipline and personal strength. You develop in yourself the iron quality of success, the one quality that will carry you forward and over any obstacle that life can throw in your path.

The Common Quality of Success in History

The history of the human race is the story of the triumph of persistence. Every great man or woman has had to endure tremendous trials and tribulations before reaching the heights of success and achievement. That endurance and perseverance is what made them great.

Winston Churchill is considered by many to have been the greatest statesman of the twentieth century. Throughout his life, he was known and respected for his courage and persistence. During the darkest hours of World War II, when the German *Luftwaffe* was bombing Britain and England stood alone, Churchill's resolute, bulldog tenacity inspired the whole nation to fight on in the face of what many felt was inevitable defeat. John F. Kennedy said of his speeches that, "Churchill marshaled the English language and sent it forward into battle."

One of the greatest speeches in the annals of persistence was Churchill's address to the nation on June 4, 1940, which ended with these words, "We shall not flag or fail . . . We shall fight in France, we shall fight on the seas and oceans, we shall fight with growing confidence and growing strength in the air, we shall defend our island, whatever the cost may be, we shall fight on the beaches, we shall fight on the landing grounds. We shall fight in the fields and in the streets, we shall fight in the hills; we shall never surrender."

In the later years of his life, Churchill was asked to address a class at his old preparatory school and share with the young people present what he believed to be the secret of his great success in life. He stood before the assembly, leaning on his cane, shaking a little, and said with a strong voice, "I can summarize the lessons of my life in seven words: never give in; never, never give in."

Your Guarantee of Eventual Success

What Churchill found, and what you will discover as you move upward and onward toward your goals, is that persistence is the one quality that guarantees you will eventually win.

Calvin Coolidge, a president who was so reluctant to speak in public that he was given the nickname of "Silent Cal," will go down in history for his simple but memorable words on this subject. He wrote, "Press on. Nothing in the world can take the place of persistence. Talent will not; nothing is more common than unsuccessful men with talent. Genius will not; unrewarded genius is almost a proverb. Education alone will not; the world is full of educated derelicts. Persistence and determination alone are omnipotent."

Persistence Is the Hallmark of Success

Successful businesspeople and entrepreneurs are all characterized by indomitable willpower and unshakable persistence.

In 1895, America was in the grip of a terrible depression. A man living in the Midwest lost his hotel in the midst of this depression and decided to write a book to motivate and inspire others to persist and carry on in spite of the difficulties facing the nation.

His name was Orison Swett Marden. He took a room above a livery stable and for an entire year he worked night and day writing a book, which he entitled *Pushing to the Front*. Late one evening, he finally finished the last page of his book and, being tired and hungry, he went down the street to a small café for dinner. While he was away for an hour, the livery stable caught on fire. By the time he got back, his entire manuscript, more than eight hundred pages, had been destroyed by the flames.

Nonetheless, drawing on his inner resources, he sat down and spent another year writing the book over again. When the book was finished, he offered it to various publishers, but no one seemed to be interested in a motivational book with the country in such a depression and unemployment so high. He then moved to Chicago and took another job. One day he mentioned this manuscript to a friend of his who happened to know a publisher. The book, *Pushing to the Front,* was subsequently published and became the runaway best-seller in the nation.

Pushing to the Front was acclaimed by the leading businesspeople and politicians in America as being the book that brought America into the twentieth century. It exerted an enormous impact on the minds of decision makers throughout the country and became the single greatest classic in all of personal development. People like Henry Ford, Thomas Edison, Harvey Firestone, and J. P. Morgan all read this book and were inspired by it.

The Two Essential Qualities

Orison Swett Marden says in his book that "There are two essential requirements for success. The first is 'get-to-it-iveness,' and the second is 'stick-to-it-iveness.'" He wrote, "No, there is no failure for the man who realizes his power, who never knows when he is beaten; there is no failure for the determined endeavor; the unconquerable will. There is no failure for the man who gets up every time he falls, who rebounds like a rubber ball, who persists when everyone else gives up, who pushes on when everyone else turns back."

Confucius said, more than four thousand years ago, "Our greatest glory is not in never falling, but in rising every time we fall."

James J. Corbett, one of the first world heavyweight boxing champions, said that "You become a champion by fighting one more round. When things are tough, you fight one more round." Yogi Berra said this: "It ain't over 'til it's over." And the fact is that it's never over as long as you continue to persist.

Elbert Hubbard wrote, "There is no failure except in no longer trying. There is no defeat except from within, no really insurmountable barrier save our own inherent weakness of purpose."

Vince Lombardi said, "It's not whether you get knocked down. It's whether you get up again."

All of these successful men had learned how critical the quality of persistence is in achieving greater goals and objectives. Successful men and women are hallmarked by their incredible persistence, by their refusal to quit no matter what the external circumstances. The one quality that absolutely guarantees success in business, in financial accumulation, and in life is this indomitable willpower and the willingness to stick with it when everything in you wants to stop and rest or go back and do something else.

Persistence Is Your Greatest Asset

Perhaps your greatest asset is simply your ability to keep at it longer than anyone else. B. C. Forbes, the founder of *Forbes* magazine, who built it into a major publication during the darkest days of the Depression, wrote, "History has demonstrated that the most notable winners usually encountered heartbreaking obstacles before they triumphed. They won because they refused to become discouraged by their defeat."

John D. Rockefeller, at one time the richest self-made man in the world, wrote, "I do not think there is any other quality so essential to success of any kind, as the quality of perseverance. It overcomes almost everything, even nature."

Conrad Hilton, who started with a dream and a small hotel in Lubbock, Texas, and went on to build one of the most successful hotel corporations in the world, said, "Success seems to be connected with action. Successful men keep moving. They make mistakes, but they don't quit."

Thomas Edison, the greatest *failure*, and also the greatest *success*, in the history of invention, failed at more experiments than any other inventor of the twentieth century. He also perfected and was granted more patents for commercial processes than any other inventor of his age. He described his philosophy in these words: "When I have fully decided that a result is worth getting, I go ahead on it and make trial after trial until it comes. Nearly every man who develops an idea, works it up to the point where it looks impossible and then gets discouraged. That's not the place to become discouraged."

Alexander Graham Bell talked about persistence in these words: "What this power is I cannot say; all I know is that it exists and it becomes available only when a man is in that state of mind in which he knows exactly what he wants and is fully determined not to quit until he finds it."

Ren McPherson, who built build Dana Corporation into one of the great American success stories, summarized his philosophy by saying, "You just keep pushing. You just keep pushing. I made every mistake that could be made, but I just kept pushing."

The Great Paradox

An interesting and important paradox in life that you need to be aware of is that if you are an intelligent person, you do everything possible to organize your life in such a way that you minimize and avoid adversity and disappointment. This is a sensible and rational thing to do. All intelligent people, following the path of least resistance to achieve their goals, do everything possible to minimize the number of difficulties and obstacles that they will face in their day-to-day activities.

Disappointment Is Inevitable

Yet, in spite of our best efforts, disappointments and adversity are normal and natural, unavoidable parts of life. Benjamin Franklin said that the only things that are inevitable are death and taxes, but every bit of experience shows that disappointment is also inevitable. No matter how well you organize yourself and your activities, you will experience countless disappointments, setbacks, obstacles, and adversity over the course of your life. And the higher and more challenging the goals you set for yourself, the more disappointment and adversity you will experience.

This is the paradox. It is impossible for us to evolve, grow, and develop to our full potential unless we face adversity and learn from it. All of the great lessons of life come as the result of setbacks and temporary defeats, which we have done our utmost to avoid. Adversity therefore comes unbidden in spite of our best efforts. And yet without it, we cannot grow into the kind of people who are capable of scaling the heights and achieving great goals.

Adversity Is What Tests Us

Throughout history, great thinkers have reflected on this paradox and have concluded that adversity is the test that you must pass on the path to accomplishing anything worthwhile. Herodotus, the Greek philosopher, said, "Adversity has the effect of drawing out strength and qualities of a man that would have lain dormant in its absence."

The very best qualities of strength, courage, character, and persistence are brought out in you when you face your greatest challenges and you respond to them positively and constructively.

Everyone faces difficulties every step of the way. The difference between high achievers and low achievers is simply that high achievers utilize adversity and struggles for growth, while low achievers allow difficulties and adversity to overwhelm them and leave them discouraged and dejected.

Bounce Back from Disappointment

The work by Abraham Zaleznik at Harvard proved that the way you respond to disappointment is usually an accurate predictor of how likely you are to achieve great success. If you respond to disappointment by learning the very most from it and then by putting it behind you and pressing forward, you are very likely to accomplish great things in the course of your life.

Success Comes One Step Beyond Failure

This is another remarkable discovery. Your greatest successes almost invariably come one step beyond the point where everything inside of you says to quit. Men and women throughout history have been amazed to find that their great breakthroughs came about as a result of persisting in the face of all disappointment and all evidence to the contrary. This final act of persistence, which is often called the "persistence test," seems to precede great achievements of all kinds.

H. Ross Perot, who started EDS Industries with $1,000 and built it into a fortune of almost $3 billion, is one of the most successful self-made entrepreneurs in American history. He said this: "Most people give up just when they are about to achieve success. They quit on the one-yard line. They give up at the last minute of the game, one foot away from the winning touchdown."

Herodotus also wrote, *"Some men give up their designs when they have almost reached the goal; while others, on the contrary, obtain a victory by exerting, at the last moment, more vigorous efforts than ever before."*

You find this principle of persistence, of keeping on, in the life and work of countless great men and women. Florence Scovel Shinn wrote that, "Every great work, every big accomplishment, has been brought into manifestation through holding to the vision, and often just before the big achievement comes apparent failure and discouragement."

Napoleon Hill, in his classic, *Think and Grow Rich*, wrote, "Before success comes in any man's life, he is sure to meet with much temporary defeat and, perhaps, some failure. When defeat overtakes a man, the easiest and most logical thing to do is quit. And that is exactly what the majority of men and women do."

Harriet Beecher Stowe, who wrote *Uncle Tom's Cabin,* also wrote these words, "Never give up then, for that is just the place and time that the tide will turn."

What you do not see—what most people never suspect of existing—is the silent but irresistible power that comes to your rescue when you fight on in the face of discouragement.

Claude M. Bristol wrote, "It's the constant and determined effort that breaks down all resistance, sweeps away all obstacles."

James Whitcomb Riley put it this way, "The most essential factor is persistence—the determination never to allow your energy or enthusiasm to be dampened by the discouragement that must inevitably come."

The power to hold on in spite of everything, to endure—this is the winner's quality. Persistence is the ability to face defeat again and again without giving up—to push on in the face of great difficulty. There is a poem by an anonymous author that I think everyone should read and memorize and recite to himself or herself when tempted to quit or to stop trying. This poem is called "Don't Quit."

Don't Quit

When things go wrong, as they sometimes will.
When the road you're trudging seems all up hill.
When the funds are low and the debts are high.
And you want to smile, but you have to sigh.
When care is pressing you down a bit.
Rest, if you must, but don't you quit.
Life is queer with its twists and turns.
As every one of us sometimes learns.
And many a failure turns about
When he might have won had he stuck it out:
Don't give up though the pace seems slow—

You may succeed with another blow.
Success is failure turned inside out—
The silver tint of the clouds of doubt.
And you never can tell how close you are.
It may be near when it seems so far:
So stick to the fight when you're hardest hit—
It's when things seem worst that you must not QUIT.

⊞ PERSIST UNTIL YOU SUCCEED

1 Identify the biggest challenge or problem facing you today on the way to achieving your biggest goal. Imagine that it has been sent to test your resolve and desire. Decide that you will never give up.

2 Think back over your life and identify the occasions where your determination to persist was the key to your success. Remind yourself of those experiences whenever you face difficulties or discouragement of any kind.

3 Resolve in advance that as long as you intensely desire your goal, you will never give up until you achieve it.

4 Look into every problem, difficulty, obstacle, or setback for the seed of an equal or greater benefit or opportunity. You will always find something that can help you.

5 In every situation, resolve to be solution oriented and action oriented. Think always in terms of what you can do right now to solve your problems or achieve your goals and then get started! Never give up.

⬚ | Conclusion

Take Action Today

You have now learned perhaps the most comprehensive strategy for setting and achieving goals that has ever been put together in one book. By practicing these rules and principles, you can accomplish more in the coming months and years than most people accomplish in a lifetime.

The most important quality you can develop for lifelong success is the habit of taking action on your plans, goals, ideas, and insights. The more often you try, the sooner you will triumph. There is a direct relationship between the number of things you attempt and your accomplishments in life. Here are the twenty-one steps for setting and achieving goals and for living a wonderful life.

1. Unlock Your Potential—Always remember that your true potential is unlimited. Whatever you have accomplished in life up to now has only been preparation for the amazing things you can accomplish in the future.

2. Take Charge of Your Life—You are completely responsible for everything you are today, for everything you think, say, and do, and for everything you become from this moment forward. Refuse to make excuses or to blame others. Instead, make progress toward your goals every day.

3. Create Your Own Future—Imagine that you have no limitations on what you can do, be, or have in the months and years ahead. Think about and plan your future as if you had all the resources you needed to create any life that you desire.

4. Clarify Your Values—Your innermost values and convictions define you as a person. Take the time to think through what you really believe in and care about in each area of your life. Refuse to deviate from what you feel is right for you.

5. Determine Your True Goals—Decide for yourself what you really want to accomplish in every area of your life. Clarity is essential for happiness and high-performance living.

6. Decide upon Your Major Definite Purpose—You need a central purpose to build your life around. There must be a single goal that will help you to achieve your other goals more than any other. Decide what it is for you and work on it all the time.

7. Analyze Your Beliefs—Your beliefs about your own abilities and about the world around you will have more of an impact on your feelings and actions than any other factor. Make sure that your beliefs are positive and consistent with achieving everything that is possible for you.

8. Start at the Beginning—Do a careful analysis of your starting point before you set off toward the achievement of your goal. Determine your exact situation today and be both honest and realistic about what you want to accomplish in the future.

9. Measure Your Progress—Set clear benchmarks, measures, and scorecards for yourself on the road to your goals. These measures help you to assess how well you are doing and enable you to make necessary adjustments and corrections as you go along.

10. Remove the Roadblocks—Success boils down to the ability to solve problems and remove obstacles on the path to your goal. Fortunately, problem solving is a skill you can master with practice and thereby achieve your goals faster than you ever thought possible.

11. Become an Expert in Your Field—You have within you, right now, the ability to be one of the very best at what you do, to join the top 10 percent in your field. Set this as a goal, work on it every day, and never stop working at it until you get there.

12. Associate with the Right People—Your choices of people with whom to live, work, and socialize will have more of an effect on your success than any other factor. Resolve today to associate only with people you like, respect, and admire. Fly with the eagles if you want to be an eagle yourself.

13. Make a Plan of Action—An ordinary person with a well-thought-out plan will run circles around a genius without one. Your ability to plan and organize in advance will enable you to accomplish even the biggest and most complex goals.

14. Manage Your Time Well—Learn how to double and triple your productivity, performance, and output by practicing practical and proven time management principles. Always set priorities before you begin and then concentrate on the most valuable use of your time.

15. Review Your Goals Daily—Take time every day, every week, every month to review and reevaluate your goals and objectives. Make sure that you are still on track and that you are still working toward what is important to you. Be prepared to modify your goals and plans with new information.

16. Visualize Your Goals Continually—Direct the movies of your mind. Your imagination is your preview of your life's coming attractions. Repeatedly "see" your goals as if they already existed. Your clear, exciting mental images activate all your mental powers and attract your goals into your life.

17. Activate Your Superconscious Mind—You have within you and around you an incredible power that will bring you everything and anything you want or need. Take the time regularly to tap into this amazing source of ideas and insights for goal attainment.

18. Remain Flexible at All Times—Be clear about your goal but be flexible about the process of achieving it. Be constantly open to new, better, faster, cheaper ways to achieve the same result, and if something is not working, be willing to try a different approach.

19. Unlock Your Inborn Creativity—You have more creative ability to solve problems and come up with new and better ways for goal attainment than you have ever used. You are a potential genius. You can tap into your intelligence to overcome any obstacle and achieve any goal you can set for yourself.

20. Do Something Every Day—Use the "Momentum Principle of Success" by getting started toward your goal and then doing something every day that moves you closer to what you want to accomplish. Action orientation is essential to your success.

21. Persist until You Succeed—In the final analysis, your ability to persist longer than anyone else is the one quality that will guarantee great success in life. Persistence is self-discipline in action and the true measure of your belief in yourself. Resolve in advance that you will *never, never* give up!

There they are, the twenty-one most important principles of goal setting and goal achieving ever discovered. Your regular review and practice of these principles will enable you to live an extraordinary life. Nothing can stop you now.

Good luck!

Recommended Reading

The Achievement Factors. B. Eugene Griessman.
The Achiever's Profile. Allan Cox.
Achieving Peak Performance. Nido Qubein.
The Acorn Principle. Jim Cathcart.
Advanced Selling Strategies. Brian Tracy.
Adversity Quotient. Paul G. Stolz.
The Art of Negotiating. Gerald Nierenberg.
Breakpoint and Beyond. George Land and Beth Jarman.
Breathing Space. Jeff Davidson.
Built to Last. James C. Collins and Jerry I. Porras.
The Business of Selling. Tony Alessandra and Jim Cathcart.
Competing in the Third Wave. Jeremy Hope and Tony Hope.
Consultative Selling. Mack Hanan.
Creating Wealth. Robert G. Allen.
Creating Your Future. George Morrisey.
Customer Intimacy. Fred Wiersema.
Customers for Life. Carl Sewell.
Do What You Love, the Money Will Follow. Marsha Sinetar.
Economics in One Lesson. Henry Hazlitt.
The Effective Executive. Peter F. Drucker.
Essays. Ralph Waldo Emerson.
The Experience Economy. B. Joseph Tine II and James H. Gilmore.
Fast-Growth Management. Mack Hanan.
Faust. Johann Wolfgang von Goethe.
The Feldman Method. Andrew H. Thomson and Lee Roster.
The Fifth Discipline. Peter Senge.
Flow: The Psychology of Optimal Experience. Mihalay
  Csiksczentmihalyi.
Getting Everything You Can out of All You've Got. Jay Abraham.
The Great American Success Story. George Gallup Jr.
  and Alec N. Gallup.
Henderson on Corporate Strategy. Bruce Henderson.
How to Win Customers. Heinz Goldman.
Hyper Growth. H. Skip Weitzen.

Innovation and Entrepreneurship. Peter F. Drucker.
Job Shift. William Bridges.
Key Management Ideas. Stuart Crainer.
The Law of Success. Napoleon Hill.
Leadership. James J. Cribbin.
The Leadership Challenge. James M. Kouzes and Barry C. Posner.
Leadership When the Heat's On. Danny Cox.
Leading People. Robert H. Rosen.
Life beyond Time Management. Kim Norup and Willy Norup.
Lifetime Guide to Money. Wall Street Journal.
Locus of Control. Herbert M. Lefcourt.
The Management of Time. James T. McKay.
Managing for Results. Peter F. Drucker.
Managing the Future. Robert B. Tucker.
Man's Search for Meaning. Victor Frankl.
The Marketing Imagination. Theodore Leavitt.
Maximum Achievement. Brian Tracy.
Megatrends 2000. John Naisbitt and Patricia Aburdene.
Million Dollar Habits. Robert Ringer.
The Negotiators Handbook. George Fuller.
Nicomachian Ethics. Aristotle.
Nobody Gets Rich Working for Somebody Else. Roger Fritz.
Og Mandino's University of Success. Og Mandino.
On Becoming a Leader. Warren Bennis.
Only the Paranoid Survive. Andrew S. Grove.
The Organized Executive. Stephanie Winston.
Organized to Be the Best. Susan Silver.
Outperformers. Mack Hanan.
Passion for Excellence. Tom Peters and Nancy Austin.
The Path of Least Resistance. Robert Fritz.
Pathfinders. Gayle Sheehy.
Peak Performers. Charles Garfield.
Permission Marketing. Seth Godin.
Play to Win. Larry Wilson.
Positioning. Al Reis and Jack Trout.
Power in Management. John P. Cotter.
The Power of Purpose. Richard J. Leider.
The Power of Simplicity. Jack Trout.
The Practice of Management. Peter F. Drucker.
Price Wars. Thomas J. Winninger.

Profit Patterns. Adrian J. Slywotzky and David J. Morrison.
Pushing the Envelope. Harvey Mackay.
Pygmalion in the Classroom. Dr. Robert Rosenthal.
Quality Is Free. Phillip Crosby.
Quality without Tears. Phillip Crosby.
Real Time. Regis McKenna.
Relationship Selling. Jim Cathcart.
Richest Man in Babylon. George Classon.
The Sale. Don Hutson.
Secrets of Effective Leadership. F. A. Manske Jr.
Sell Easy. Thomas J. Winninger.
Selling the Invisible. Harry Beckwith.
Servant Leadership. Robert K. Greenleaf.
The Seven Habits of Highly Effective People. Stephen Covey.
The Situational Leader. Dr. Paul Hersey.
The Soul of a Business. Tom Chappell.
Stress without Distress. Hans Selye.
Success Is a Journey. Brian Tracy.
The Success Principle. Ronald N. Yeaple.
TechnoTrends. Daniel Burrus.
The Unheavenly City. Dr. Edward Banfield.
Think and Grow Rich. Napoleon Hill.
The Time Trap. Alex Mackenzie.
Top Management Strategy. Benjamin B. Tregoe
   and John W. Zimmerman.
The 22 Immutable Laws of Branding. Al Reis and Laura Reis.
The 22 Immutable Laws of Marketing. Al Reis and Jack Trout.
Visionary Leadership. Bert Mannus.
Visions. Ty Boyd.
Wealth without Risk. Charles J. Givens.
Working Smart. Michael LeBoeuf.
You Can Negotiate Anything. Herb Cohen.
The Zurich Axioms. Max Gunther.

Learning Resources of Brian Tracy International

BRIAN TRACY'S PERSONAL COACHING PROGRAMS

The Keys to Making a Quantum Leap in Your Life and Career

Focal Point Advanced Coaching
and Mentoring Program

Brian Tracy offers a personal coaching program in San Diego for successful entrepreneurs, self-employed professionals, and top salespeople. Participants learn how to apply the Focal Point Process to every part of their work and personal lives.

Personal Strategic Planning—Participants learn a step-by-step process of personal strategic planning that enables them to take complete control of their time and their lives. Over the course of the program, participants meet with Brian Tracy one full day every three months. During these sessions, they learn how to double their income and double their time off.

Focus and Concentration—Participants identify what they enjoy doing the most and learn how to become better in their most profitable activities. They learn how to delegate, downsize, eliminate, and get rid of all the tasks they neither enjoy nor benefit from. They learn how to identify their special talents and how to use leverage and concentration to move to the top of their fields.

Focal Point Personal Telephone Coaching Program

Brian Tracy's personally trained professional coaches work with you step by step to help you move to the next level of performance in your career.

Twelve-Part Program—This intensive twelve-week program comes complete with exercises, audio programs, pre-work, and personalized coaching.

Personal Accountability—You learn how to implement the Focal Point Process in every area of your life. Working with a trusted mentor, you develop complete clarity about who you are, what you want, where you are going, and the fastest ways to achieve all your goals.

❖

For more information on the live or telephone
coaching and mentoring programs offered by
Brian Tracy, visit www.briantracy.com,
call 858-481-2977, or write to Brian Tracy International,
462 Stevens Avenue, Suite 202, Solana Beach, CA 92075.

Visit Brian Tracy at www.21successsecrets.com
for a free copy of his audio program,
"The 21 Success Secrets of Self-Made Millionaires."
You pay only shipping and handling!

Also, check out some of Brian Tracy's other books,
Eat That Frog! and *The 100 Absolutely Unbreakable Laws of Business Success*, at your local bookstore or
at www.briantracy.com.

BRIAN TRACY
SPEAKER • AUTHOR • TRAINER

Brian Tracy is one of the most popular professional speakers in the world. He addresses more than 250,000 people each year in talks and seminars, from keynote addresses to sessions three to four days in length.

His topics include

- High Performance Leadership for the 21st Century
- Maximizing Personal Performance
- Advanced Selling Skills and Strategies
- Counter Attack! for Salespeople and Businesses

For more information, visit www.briantracy.com. Register for a free subscription to one or more of Brian's helpful newsletters on Personal Success, Time Management, and Financial Mastery.

To book Brian as a speaker, contact
Brian Tracy International
462 Stevens Avenue, Suite 202
Solana Beach, CA 92075
Phone 858-481-2977, x17
Fax 858-481-2445
www.briantracy.com

Visit **www.briantracy.com** and
sign up for a **Free Subscription** to
Brian's personal Sales Success Newsletter!

Index

abilities, 89~90, 100~101, 109, 130~131, 142

achievers/achievements, 36~37, 123, 152~153

acting "as if," 77~78. See also Law of Correspondence

action orientation, 36~37, 244, 252, 262, 274~277

action planning, 276; assembling teams, 157~158; bottlenecks, 159~160; creating your plan, 150; critical results, 160; discipline of, 155; formula for success, 153~154; importance of process, 151; limiting factors, 156; listing tasks/activities, 155; master skill of success, 149; payoff of, 152; priorities/sequences, 155~156; process as key, 151~152; savings of, 153; solution orientation for, 157

actions, 41, 44, 81, 185, 211

activities, 104~105, 155~156, 163~164, 165, 172, 260, 277. See also tasks

Adler, Alfred, 73, 205

analyses, 104~105, 115~116, 128~129, 257~258, 275

Asagioli, Roberto, 205

assets, 91~92, 268~269

attaining goals: activating forces in the universe, 184; discipline, 182; doubling speed of, 176~177; just doing it, 184~185; mental programming, 186~187; multiplying results, 185; setting deadlines, 181~182; subconscious mind, 180~181, 183~184; systematic versus random goal setting, 178; Ten Goal Exercise, 180; Three P Formula, 180; trusting the process, 182~183; using index cards, 185~186; writing goals down daily, 178~179

attitudes, 24, 41, 107~108, 145, 245, 255, 256~257

"balanced scorecard," 99~100

Banfield, Edward, 31

behavior, 43~44, 46, 80

beliefs: acquired versus inborn, 75; acting

your way into feeling, 77~78; behaving consistently with self-image, 80; changing your thinking, 71; consistency of words/actions, 81; creating mental equivalents, 79~80; decision making, 80~81; different intelligences and genius, 74~75; ignoring experts about, 72~73; inferiority, 73~74; Law of Belief, 70; looking for the good, 77; master program for success, 71~72; secret of sales manager example, 78~79; selecting the ones you want, 76~77; self-limiting, 72~73, 75, 81; subjective nature of, 72; thinking of yourself differently, 75~76; values and, 41

Billings, Josh, 75

Bismarck, Otto von, 240~241

blaming others, 21~23

bosses, 138~139

brain, and creativity, 227~228

Bristol, Claude M., 272

Buzan, Tony, 227

career moves, 125~126, 246

Cathcart, Jim, 130, 190

changes: in circumstances, 88~89; controlling direction of, 14; factors that drive, 217; flexibility and speed of, 216; making necessary, 88; in your thinking, 71

changing your mind, 222~223

character development, 193~194, 263

choosing wisely, 169, 170

Churchill, Winston, 254, 264~265

clarity, 12~15, 50. See also values clarification; for determining your true goals, 59; and flexibility, 225; of goals, 200; of long-term goals, 164~165; of your major definite purpose, 64; of your value, 171

closure, 97~98, 100

Collins, Jim, 92~93

comfort zones, 114, 219~220

"Compensation" (Emerson), 245

constraints, 110. See also roadblocks, removing

control, 14, 27~28

285

About the Author

Brian Tracy is one of the top professional speakers and trainers in the world today. He addresses more than 250,000 men and women each year on the subjects of leadership, strategy, sales, and personal and business success.

Brian is an avid student of business, psychology, management, sales, history, economics, politics, metaphysics, and religion. He brings a unique blend of humor, insight, information, and inspiration to the more than 100 talks and seminars he conducts worldwide each year.

Brian believes that each person has extraordinary untapped potential that he or she can learn to access and, in so doing, accomplish more in a few years than the average person does in a lifetime.

Brian Tracy is the chairman of Brian Tracy International, a human resource development company headquartered in Solana Beach, California. He has written sixteen books and produced more than 300 audio and video training programs. His materials have been translated into twenty languages and are used in thirty-eight countries.

Brian lives with his wife, Barbara, and their four children in Solana Beach, California. He is active in community affairs and serves as a consultant to several nonprofit organizations.

Eat That Frog!
21 Great Ways to Stop Procrastinating and Get More Done in Less Time

Using "eat that frog" as a metaphor for tackling the most challenging task of your day—the one you are most likely to procrastinate on, but also probably the one that can have the greatest positive impact on your life—*Eat That Frog!* helps you stop procrastinating and get more things done faster.

Hardcover • ISBN 1-58376-202-7 • Item #62027 $19.95
Paperback • ISBN 1-57675-198-8 • Item #51988 $13.95

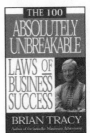

The 100 Absolutely Unbreakable Laws of Business Success

In this eye-opening practical guide, renowned business speaker and author Brian Tracy presents a set of principles or "universal laws" that lie behind the success of business people everywhere. You will learn how to attract and keep better people, produce and sell more, improve products and services, control costs more intelligently, expand and grow more predictably, and increase your profits.

Paperback • ISBN 1-57675-126-0 • Item #51260 $15.95
Hardcover • ISBN 1-57675-107-4 • Item #51074 $24.95
Audiocassette, 4 cassettes/6 hours • ISBN 1-57453-380-0
Item #33800 $25.00

Be a Sales Superstar
21 Great Ways to Sell More, Faster, Easier in Tough Markets

In this concise and action-oriented handbook Brian Tracy shares the most important principles for sales success. *Be a Sales Superstar* is for busy sales professionals, providing key ideas and techniques that will immediately increase your effectiveness and boost your results.

Hardcover • ISBN 1-57675-175-9 • Item #51759 $19.95
Paperback • ISBN 1-57675-273-9 • Item #52739 $14.95

Berrett-Koehler Publishers
PO Box 565, Williston, VT 05495-9900
Call toll-free! **800-929-2929** 7 am-9 pm EST

Or fax your order to 1-802-864-7626
For fastest service order online: **www.bkconnection.com**

Spread the word!